CONFRONTING COMPANY POLITICS

Confronting Company Politics

Beverley Stone

MACMILLAN
Business

First published 1997 by
MACMILLAN PRESS LTD
Houndmills, Basingstoke, Hampshire RG21 6XS
and London
Companies and representatives
throughout the world

ISBN 0–333–68154–1

A catalogue record for this book is available
from the British Library.

This book is printed on paper suitable for recycling and
made from fully managed and sustained forest sources.

10   9   8   7   6   5   4   3   2   1
06   05   04   03   02   01   00   99   98   97

Copy-edited and typeset by Povey–Edmondson
Tavistock and Rochdale, England

Printed and bound in Great Britain by
Creative Print and Design (Wales), Ebbw Vale

It took me a long time to realise that my parents were different. They encouraged me and my three brothers to trust ourselves, question authority, be honest, stay focused, be courageous and act. They encouraged us to live an existential life. They also believed with all their hearts that the main purpose of every adult is to make the world a better place for the next generation and they worked hard towards this end. My mother, whom I admire greatly, continues to do so. This book is therefore dedicated to mum and dad and to my wonderful and authentic daughters, Zelda and Becky, our future generation of existential change agents.

Contents

Acknowledgements

This book consists of my reflections on organisational life which began as an 'outsider' at nursery school as I watched and wondered at the leadership style and resultant climate of the teachers and headmistress! So first I wish to thank all those with whom I have had the fortune or misfortune to learn, work or socialise with, especially those who have been so honest and open about their feelings and thoughts during the years.

I am particularly grateful to Eric Hall and Arthur Worster who helped me travel the uncomfortable path from my first science-oriented degree to their experiential master's degree where all my intuitions and philosophical readings started to take on a pragmatic shape in the form of existential psychology.

I also want to thank my brother Brian and sister-in-law Linda for their empathy and encouragement, particularly in providing their home for a couple of weeks which gave me the peace I needed to break the back of the book. And my brother Andrew for his unswerving faith in my ability and continual support. And my brother Robert who, though I was a late starter in academia, always had faith in my common sense.

The completion of this book would have been much more painful had I not had the help of Peter Scawen in my last month of writing when the mere thought of completing the final chapters left my whole mind and body screaming "Who Cares"! Not only did Peter help me remain convinced that what I had to say was worth saying but he hung in there day after day as a sounding board, either paraphrasing my excited ramblings, working through our mutual client experiences to illustrate points or giving me the encouragement to stop anaesthetising my well-worn phrases in the attempt to make them sound more 'literary'. Peter also spent many hours transferring my models to the PC, still a source of wonder to me, and reading through the manuscript providing reminders and observations which I invariably incorporated into the book.

I am sincerely grateful to Stephen Rutt, my editor whose advice was so spot on that each time I received some feedback it provided me with the spurt of enthusiasm I needed to continue writing.

Finally, I want to thank my mother, Zelda, Becky, my clients and my many colleagues who by ceaselessly asking 'Have you written the book yet?' encouraged me to do so at last. One less regret on my deathbed!

BEVERLEY STONE

1 Is Company Politics Strangling Your Business, and You With It?

‘The hardest battle is to be nobody but yourself in a world which is doing its best, night and day, to make you everybody else.’

(*e.e. cummings*)

The nature of company politics

The term ‘company politics’ refers to all the game-playing, snide, ‘them and us’, aggressive, sabotaging, negative, blaming, ‘win-lose’, withholding, non-cooperative behaviour that goes on in hundreds of interactions everyday in your organisation. Those who indulge in company politics do so in order to achieve their *personal agenda* at the expense of others in the organisation. In the process, they demoralise the motivated and sabotage the company's success. Given their limited numbers, like one or two bad apples souring the whole barrel, they are disproportionately powerful.

Personal agendas are usually called ‘hidden agendas’, even though they are rarely, if ever, hidden! Everyone knows certain individuals who consistently act out of their personal agendas and how this influences the tone, content and outcome of discussions, meetings and task accomplishment. Yet, when individuals fail to get an honest opinion, cooperative response or a straight answer from a so-called colleague, rather than deal with the personal agenda, they prefer to avoid confrontation and instead express their anger, frustration and powerlessness in ‘corridor meetings’ with friends.

Both the company politics and the unwillingness to confront them result in an *organisation culture*, characterised by:

- Low morale
- Internal competition
- Mistrust

1

- Lack of communication
- Top management non-cooperation
- Interdepartmental conflict
- Inaccessibility of the MD
- Lack of strong, cohesive leadership
- Feelings of powerlessness.

Traditional attempts to change the culture by empowering individuals have relied on developing a supportive, communicative and cooperative environment where people feel safe to use their creative potential in the pursuit of organisational goals. Though successful in the short term, this approach usually results in the company reverting back to the old culture in the long term, reaffirming everyone's original sense of powerlessness.

The alternative approach developed in this book is to help individuals take personal responsibility for consistently **confronting company politics in a hostile environment.** This existential approach not only encourages them to recognise that they have the power to change their external environment by choosing to take risks but also challenges them to consider their own part in the difficulties they are having.

Existentialism empowers by showing individuals that they are their own jailer. Even though the quality of their working lives and freedom to reach their optimum performance is severely limited by the pressures inside the organisation, individuals are not merely victims of circumstances beyond their control. They are responsible for the consequences not only of what they do but also what they fail to do. For example, what they may *do* is blame others for not creating a safe environment; what they may *fail to do* is act themselves.

Culture-change programmes need to reverse the process. First company politics needs to be confronted and eliminated or its effects severely constrained, even when the environment is unsupportive, uncommunicative and uncooperative. It is this which will lead to the creation of a safe environment, long-term change and increased productivity, revenue and profit.

Organisation culture and company politics

In an attempt to change the old culture Organisation Development consultants, both internal and external, have, for the past 15 years at least, advocated the creation of an 'excellent culture'. An 'excellent culture' is one where the senior management team has agreed, committed to and published a mission or vision (a common goal) along with the values, attitudes and beliefs that they expect of themselves and others. These define the 'oughts' of behaviour, the *behavioural norms*, within and between working groups, which they expect to colour the daily activities of those working in the organisation.

Excellent cultures have *positive behavioural norms* that support the organisation's goals and objectives and encourage cooperative behaviour directed toward their achievement. Examples include norms that value a sense of urgency, hard work, loyalty, a 'customer-first' mentality, pride, a sense of belonging, recognition, achievement, personal development, quality consciousness, personal responsibility, trust, openness, creative risk-taking, autonomy, professionalism, and a willingness to seek and implement change.

In most culture-change programmes Departmental Managers agree to not only live by these values, attitudes and behaviours but also to reward and encourage them both within their own departments and between departments. Figure 1 shows this ideal culture where all departments work with each other in the same style towards a common goal.

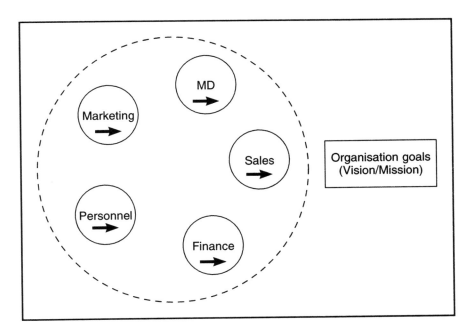

Figure 1   Departments working with the same values, attitudes and behaviours and their 'eye on the ball'

The problem is that this rarely, if ever, happens and people continue to play politics. Why? Because the focus on values, attitudes, behaviours and common goals is misplaced. An understanding and even internalisation of these *does not result in action*. The following scenario illustrates this.

We are all familiar with the project manager who has numerous reasons why a project is going to take longer, cost more and be far more complex than the sales executive, as usual, told him. The sales executive's response is to look concerned or angry, say little, disbelievingly accept the information and, once again, go and complain loudly to the rest of the sales team.

The project manager's personal agenda is to exaggerate the problem both to ensure his department's success and to get back at the sales executive for selling unrealistic promises to the customer. The sales executive's personal agenda is to minimise the problems to the customer in order to maximise his commission.

The project manager believes that all sales executives are over-optimistic and cavalier in their attitude whereas the sales executive believes that all project managers are over-pessimistic and pedestrian. The sales executive wishes that the project manager would just get on with the job whilst the project manager wishes the sales executive would just tell the truth.

During their interaction none of this is mentioned. Both avoid confronting the real issues for fear that the conflict will be uncomfortable, make the situation worse and cause each of them more problems with the customer. The subtext, which is the game being played between them, remains silent. In effect, each allows their fears to control their personal behaviour.

Both have attended a change programme, learnt the company values and attitudes, know the mission and vision and been trained in assertiveness, conflict handling and teambuildng. They have the skills, they've internalised the values but when they come face to face with game-playing, they *still don't act*.

The focus of all change programmes must surely, therefore, be on the *mechanics of action*.

Personal versus organisational goals

As a result of this reluctance to act and confront the sabotage of those pursuing their own agendas, both the original culture and the one that regrettably remains after many change programmes is one where either:

(a) There is *no common goal or vision* so that personal goals can readily override organisational ones.

(b) There is a *stated common goal or vision* but team members are *not truly committed* and so personal goals override organisational ones.

(c) There is a *truly common goal or vision* but department heads have *different values, attitudes and beliefs* regarding how to achieve it, some valuing rules, caution and control (e.g. in the Accounts Department), others valuing flexibility, speed and autonomy (e.g. in the Sales Department).

Company politics arises out of the dynamics of people fighting to carry out their work in such a way that reflects or disguises their *own* values and attitudes about how the job should be done, and how others should be treated in the process.

When there are either no shared goals or there is no agreement on how best to motivate others to achieve these goals, meetings and interactions are unfocused. Decisions are frequently made by team members lobbying, bullying or avoiding each other in order to achieve their own objectives, be they the organisation's goals, their department's objectives or personal power and control, all of which may be incompatible. This is illustrated in Figure 2.

Company politics as negative behavioural norms

Company politics, then, results in a **culture of non-cooperation** characterised overwhelmingly more by *negative behavioural norms* than by positive ones. Negative norms are those which promote behaviour that works against the achievement of the goals and objectives of the

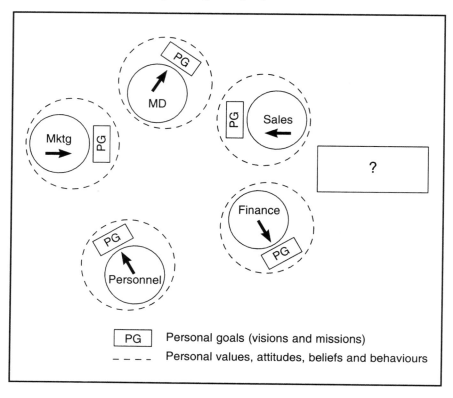

Figure 2   Departments with different values, attitudes and behaviours and no common goal

organisation. Examples include criticism of the company, blaming, negativity, distrust, absenteeism, inertia, customer indifference or disparagement, a 'them and us' relationship with management, time-wasting, interdepartmental non-cooperation and subversive entrenchment of the status quo.

When new employees join a company they soon learn the difference between the *desired* positive norms and those in *practice* and, if they want to be accepted by their peers, they quickly conform to those in practice. There is a cultural mix of those who want to adopt the desired values, attitudes and behaviours and those who, through game-playing and company politics, define and reinforce those in practice.

In most organisations you can break down the individuals into the following three categories:

1   One-third who already possess the desired values, attitudes and behaviour and hence already fit the culture
2   One-third who are willing and able to change to fit the culture
3   One-third who do not fit and will never change to fit the culture.

It is a sad reflection in terms of wasted time, money and effort that this breakdown typically remains the same both before *and* after a traditional programme of change.

Eventually, the direct or indirect aggression of the 'saboteurs' weakens the resolve of the 'motivated' until they leave either physically, or worse, psychologically. They give up on acting in accordance with their values and attitudes and the positive norms:

It's not the people who have left the organisation that we should worry about, it is the people who have 'left' but are still there!

Just imagine how much positive energy is being suppressed and diminished every minute of every day by those who have only negative intent.

When traditional culture-change programmes, that attempt to elim-inate a culture of non-cooperation by focusing on the clarification of desired values, attitudes, behaviours and goals, have demonstrably not worked, at least, in the long term, the blame for the failure has frequently been put at the feet of uncommitted managers who do not exhibit the strong leadership skills necessary to enforce and reinforce the desired values, attitudes and behaviours.

The argument for strong leadership

It is self-evidently true that if a company has incredibly strong-willed, single-minded leadership it can support those with the desired values and attitudes and turn around or tease out those without. The following are some obvious examples:

- Marks & Spencer
- The Virgin Group
- The Third Reich
- The Mirror Group
- The Thatcher government
- McDonald's
- Price Waterhouse
- IBM.

If you worked for one of them, there was little choice but to conform to their values or go.

There is nothing new in saying that leaders should encourage those with the positive norms and discourage those with the negative norms that influence so much of the business. A strong leader can call a company meeting, stand up and say quite categorically in the right tone of voice and with the right look in his eye:

> ‘One-third of you already have the right values and I will consistently support you, one-third of you can learn the values and I will take the time to develop you, and one-third of you, I suspect, will never have the right values and, whilst I'm sure you're perfectly nice people, you will either take them on board or go and find a culture that suits you better!’

Pointing to the wall he can say: 'This is my vision, mission and values. I want every one of you to act in my way to achieve our goal and I mean it. I'm off to Hong Kong.' A strong leader could then get on a plane and still empower his staff even by fax! Every decision, every plan, every action that followed would indicate and reinforce his values. He would only need one day a month in the country to prove he meant it.

For example, if, on his return from Hong Kong as he landed at Heathrow, he phoned his receptionist and she was as unpleasant as usual and he sacked her on arrival and then had a meeting, and came down heavily on those playing the old games, before leaving the same day for Japan, the two-thirds with positive norms would be buzzing. They would be well and truly convinced that he meant it and feel empowered (even by an absent leader) to work according to the new values and attitudes and confront those who did not.

The success of the 'zero tolerance' programme used by the NYPD and the experiment in Strathclyde and King's Cross, London illustrates what can be achieved by strong leaders who pick up on every minor mistake so as to infuse the entire organisation with the desired values. There is no doubt the culture follows the values of strong leadership.

Yet this leadership style is rare, since many managers do not pick up on every transgression. They don't act – they don't do what they say they'll do. The leaders themselves can be split into the three different types. There are those who have the desired values and attitudes of the CEO, those who don't have them but are flexible enough to be willing to learn, and those who are simply saboteurs by nature.

So what is the solution given that strong, single-minded, committed leadership is rare leaving most management teams and employees to flounder alone amongst the everyday battles? I don't think there is enough time to get those *without* the values to develop and internalise them so well that they will instil them into the culture every minute of every day in every action, be they in Hong Kong, a customer site or in-house. However, the good news is that in every organisation we *already have* one-third who have them and one third who are happy to take them on board.

| The central issue is not how to change a lifetime's values and attitudes but how to encourage individuals who have the desired values to *live* by them. |

All the effort in culture-change programmes has been in conveying desired values and goals. Yet change is not merely a *values* issue – it's an issue about *action*. Each individual has to become responsible for their own behaviour in dealing with each situation in which they find themselves. This can be expressed as an *existential approach*.

Individual responsibility for action

What distinguishes the existential approach from conventional change programmes is the emphasis on accepting our responsibility for every aspect of our lives, not only our *responsibility for our actions* but also our responsibility for our *inaction* in life.

Change is not just about understanding, knowing, intending and dreaming. Change must be expressed in *action*. Yet programmes of change pursue other goals – insight, mutual understanding, commonality, clarity, focus, creativity, autonomy, measurement, self-actualisation, reassurance and comfort. These may facilitate change but in the final analysis, *action* is the objective of every programme and must be the goal of every individual, every manager and every department.

The problem is that nowhere in organisation, management or personal development programmes is the focus on the *mechanics of action*. Instead we focus on *organisational issues* such as visions, missions, company structure, strategy, corporate values and attitudes, task improvements and objectives and *group process issues* such as relationships, cultures, group dynamics and feelings, in the blind hope that pursuance of these will ultimately generate change.

And when this fails everyone becomes even more blasé, cynical, suspicious, depressed, entrenched, helpless, hopeless, angry and frustrated so that management either goes back to 'command and control' or finds the next 'flavour of the month' Organisation Development panacea involving more self-scrutiny, analysis and insight.

Since the management, staff and Organisation Development specialists are not clear on how personal change is to come about, they hope that by having both more, and more open, conversations exploring more and more problems and generating more and more solutions, merely 'through the process of mutual fatigue' (A. Wheelis, in his 1956 article on 'Will and Psychoanalysis') they will stumble on an approach that works when the whole organisation will suddenly spring into action. But they don't.

Using potential in a *hostile* environment

To argue that individuals will stop playing games or being defensive if we create a climate where people feel safe to take the risk of using their creative potential is demonstrably not enough. The *safe environment does not last*, since one-third don't want it to last and the other two-thirds won't confront them. It's irrelevant whether we have employees with the desired values, attitudes, beliefs and 'eye on the ball', if as soon as they are left to their own devices they clam up and blame everyone else for it!

The real questions for organisations to consider are:

(a)   Why don't the one-third *with* the requisite values and attitudes *before* the programme live by them?

(b)   Why don't the one-third who sincerely take them on board *during* the programme live by them *after* it?

(c)   Why do the motivated leave physically or psychologically, rather than be *themselves*?

The challenge for culture-change programmes is not how to get those with undesirable values, attitudes and behaviours to change, but to find out *why* those with the desirable ones don't behave accordingly, and how we can help them *act*.

Most people say that they'd like to confront politics, but they don't dare to. Change involves not only open communication, shared goals and a 'customer-first' mentality but also the personal commitment by each individual to deal with their own 'existential issues' if they are to take the risk to:

(a)   change their *own* behaviour, and

(b)   confront those who refuse to do so, preferring to continue to play company politics.

Rather than waste more time, energy and money on establishing short-term improvements to the working environment, might not a better approach to long-term organisation change be to answer the question:

How do we enable individuals to act on their values and attitudes in a *hostile* environment?

It's a tough journey

The purpose of this book is to give individuals the skills to confront company politics by taking the risk of being themselves and living an existential life. *It's a tough journey:*

- it's tough to be free
- it's tough to make decisions
- it's tough to act on decisions
- it's tough to choose
- it's tough to be responsible for your actions and failures to act
- it's tough to travel alone.

It's tough, but it's worth it. We all have moments in our lives when we work hard, we work together and we succeed – all the pieces of the puzzle fit and we feel great.

We know the feeling when we take the risk of adopting a tough negotiating position that pays off, the risk of creating a marketing campaign that pushes the boundaries of acceptability yet works, the risk of committing to a 5-year strategic plan that gives the company a competitive edge, the risk of being honest in the team and finding that everyone is on each other's side or when we've taken all the risks and the City thinks we're one of the best. You may be asking what's tough about that? Well just remember the struggle you had to get there. *No-one makes it easy.* When you achieve any of the above you do what you believe in, in spite of the obstacles. Not only that, but frequently the opposite occurs.

We also know the feeling when the negotiation doesn't succeed because some fool from another department neglected to phone the customer or provide them with the information when you asked them to, or the marketing campaign is highly successful but the salesmen aren't following up the leads, or the strategic plan fails because it is not being followed by 2 of your 5 divisional managers, or everyone in the team feels depressed, isolated and controlled by 1 or 2 loud members who intimidate, or the City thought you *were* one of the best, but no longer does.

The quality of your ideas didn't change, but your unwillingness to confront the behaviour of others when things went wrong meant that you were not acting according to your own beliefs, being yourself and living an existential life.

Confronting company politics through existential awareness

Company politics can make organisational life miserable, unrewarding and pointless. Rather than openly confront the situation, however, individuals prefer to complain in private and thereby collude with the saboteurs in perpetuating their power and control. This book is not about changing saboteurs, neither is it just another book on culture-change programmes. This book is about enabling those *with* the right values and attitudes who already fit the desired culture to demonstrate them in their actions, despite the saboteurs.

In order to unblock the log jam created by obstructive individuals who prevent the smooth running of customer–supplier chains throughout any organisation, we must first understand and then overcome the existential and psychological blocks of those who play and, more importantly, those who *acquiesce* in company politics.

In the words of e.e. cummings:

> • The hardest battle is to be nobody but yourself in a world which is doing its best, night and day, to make you everybody else. •

2 Can Personal Responsibility be a 'Detachable Burden'?

'When I get to Heaven they will not ask me "Why were you not Moses?"

Instead they will ask "Why were you not Susya? Why did you not become what only you could have become?"'

(Rabbi Susya)

The implicit contract of a culture of non-cooperation

In many organisations the general unwillingness to confront sabotage results in meetings, interactions and relationships characterised by an *implicit contract* that dictates how those involved will behave. Table 1 is an easy guide on how to develop a culture of non-cooperation!

Table 1 The implicit contract of a culture of non-cooperation

- Don't raise the real issues
- Don't listen to each other
- Don't speak for yourself
- Don't say what you mean
- Raise issues in 'corridor meetings' rather than in the real meeting
- Don't trust anyone
- Judge everything and everyone
- Don't experiment with new behaviour
- Never take risks and don't encourage others to do so
- Don't share in decision-making
- Don't be punctual
- Don't dare to change
- Don't confront personal agendas
- Play games and manipulate
- Do not have fun
- Blame others for everything that's wrong
- Don't take responsibility for your own behaviour
- Handle conflicts with aggression or avoidance
- Don't seek consensus
- Take silence as agreement
- Make shallow agreements
- Don't stick to commitments.

These are the manifestations of company politics that most individuals experience every day of their working lives.

Effects of company politics

Company politics can have a profound influence on the success of any business as individuals become:

- *Unfocused*, with energy spent in gaining cooperation from game-players inside the organisation rather than focusing their time and energy on achieving customer satisfaction
- *Time-wasting*, discussing the latest example with co-sufferers rather than solving the problem
- *Divisive*, with 'gangs' of like-minded individuals supporting each other in the 'battle' against the 'enemy'; a typical example of such divisive behaviour is the interdepartmental stereotyping and subsequent conflict that occurs in most organisations
- *Demoralised*: the saboteurs were demoralised in the first place otherwise they wouldn't have felt the need to play games; eventually those on the receiving end feel isolated and unsupported by those in power or their staff who either choose not to be aware of, or simply are not aware of, what's going on – this results in feelings of powerlessness until they, too, end up demoralised
- *Revengeful/withdrawn*, spending time and energy on thinking and planning of ways either to get back at the saboteur(s) or to circumvent them and thereby perpetuating and entrenching all of the above in a vicious cycle that eventually becomes the company culture.

Attempts to reverse the culture

Because of the negative effects of company politics, organisations put a lot of effort into developing a **'Non-Blaming Culture'** where people are encouraged to stop playing politics, keep their 'eye on the ball' and *take responsibility for their own behaviour.*

In order to change their behaviour, these attempts have been directed at changing their *underlying values attitudes and beliefs*, seeing individuals much like the tip of an iceberg. As a colleague, Pat Murray, puts it, when someone behaves obnoxiously we accuse them of having an 'attitude problem'. All we experience is their body language, tone of voice and the things they say but we infer that, underneath the surface, they hold values, attitudes, beliefs, feelings and so on that influence the negative behaviour as shown in Figure 3.

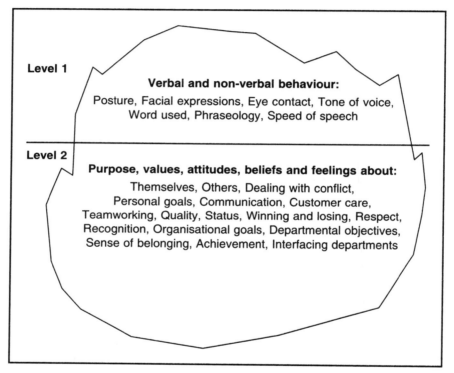

Figure 3   The 'iceberg' model of change

Literally thousands of workshops in past decades have attempted to clarify and change the values, attitudes, beliefs and feelings individuals hold about themselves and others in order to influence their communication style, group and intergroup behaviour and focus on achievement. In effect, programmes of change have attempted to redefine the implicit contract into an *explicit contract* which it is hoped will change the company culture to one where individuals feel that they can *trust* each other and have the confidence to do the actions outlined in Table 2.

Table 2   The explicit contract of a culture of cooperation

- Raise the real issues
- Listen to each other
- Speak for themselves
- Say what they mean
- Raise issues as and when they arise
- Develop a climate of trust
- Withhold judgement
- Experiment with new behaviour
- Take risks and encourage others to do so
- Share in decision-making
- Be punctual
- Dare to change
- Confront personal agendas
- Not play games and manipulate
- Have fun
- Create a non-blaming culture
- Take responsibility for their own behaviour
- Handle conflict collaboratively
- Seek consensus
- Check out silence
- Make real agreements
- Stick to commitments.

Yet these attempts at change have discovered that it's almost impossible to sustain this contract and the effective climate it induces. As anyone who's been away on a teambuilding workshop will recognise, the feelings of elation and resolve last for only a short period of time. Once back in the old environment, the pressures of work and game-playing soon contaminate all of the good intentions:

> The team spirit and resolutions made in most residential workshops are like a drop of ink in a bath – very clear and concentrated the following Monday morning but within days and weeks they dissipate until they can no longer be seen.

Such experiences are worse than not raising expectations in the first place. They only go to reinforce the *suspicion that nothing will change*, that individuals are powerless to make the change and that until senior management commits to changing *itself*, organisational life will go on in the usual turgid fashion, like trying to swim through treacle.

Blaming senior management for the fact that we won't act is not good enough. Neither is it realistic to suggest that management are impervious to the same pressures that prevent everyone else from maintaining the momentum of workshops.

So why do those who play politics continue to do so, and why don't others confront them? Why is it so difficult for everyone to maintain the explicit contract, stay open and honest, say what they mean and stick to their convictions, however unpopular?

Responsibility – a 'detachable burden'?

The central issue is the definition of the concept of *personal responsibility*. A key value in traditional culture change is that individuals 'take responsibility' for all aspects of customer care, be they internal or external customers, even if it means doing something that isn't in their job description, such as:

- answering an absent colleague's phone
- keeping the store room tidy
- putting a notice back on its hook
- smiling at clients in the waiting room
- bridging the communication gap between management and staff.

'Responsibility' here is used in the sense of 'accountability'. Each individual is as responsible as the next for doing what needs to be done in order to achieve the company vision, mission and goal. There can be *no blaming others.*

However, what generally happens is that certain individuals go to a workshop and agree to all of the content: goals, values, attitudes, beliefs, techniques and so on. They are also willing to develop self-awareness by scrutinising their own behaviour and that of the others in the group. Fired up by the empathy, warmth and enthusiasm in the group, they leave determined to change and take responsibility for their own behaviour. Yet, soon after, they go to a meeting where someone says something that doesn't fit with the new culture and they don't say a thing. As soon as the meeting finishes, they're back in a corridor meeting talking about the person who's not changed.

On their return to a follow-up workshop, some 6 weeks later, when asked if they took responsibility for their own behaviour they reply. 'No, I couldn't because no one else changed.' They blame the saboteurs once again for their despair, low energy and failure to achieve. Why?

Programmes of change are not defining the concept of responsibility in a way that encourages *real personal change*. What they *are* doing is defining 'responsibility' as follows:

> *Responsibility, n. A detachable burden easily shifted to the shoulders of G-d, Fate, Fortune, Luck or one's neighbour. In the days of astrology it was customary to unload it upon a star.*
>
> (*A. Bierce*)

In this way, 'responsibility' refers to the achievement or otherwise of *tasks*.

Responsibility – an existential definition

For existentialists, responsibility is by no means a 'detachable burden' since it refers to each individual's responsibility to be *themselves*:

> *Man is nothing else but what he makes of himself. Such is the first principle of existentialism.*
>
> (*Sartre, 1947*)

Individuals are not merely responsible for not doing the tasks but responsible for *choosing* to be passive, for *choosing* to give up their power and control, for *choosing* not to be themselves, preferring to blame others for their own behaviour.

Creating a 'non-blaming culture' involves destroying the power of those who are negative, lazy and manipulative by speaking out, saying what you think, being confrontational, being disagreed with, sticking up for what you believe in and never compromising your principles. It means both being responsible for **changing** the culture and being responsible for **avoiding** it.

As the Hassidic Rabbi Susya said, shortly before his death:

> *When I get to Heaven they will not ask me "Why were you not Moses?". Instead they will ask "Why were you not Susya? Why did you not become what only you could have become?"*
>
> (*Friedman, 1965, p. xix*)

'Responsibility' in the existential sense means that everyone in the organisation is responsible for creating their own feelings, their own suffering, their own situation and their own destiny. This means that they are free to make themselves into the kind of person they want to be and live a meaningful life. They can see this freedom either as a 'burden' which they seek to avoid or as a challenge to make something worthwhile of their lives:

To act in accordance with their values and live a meaning life, each individual must have the courage to break away from their old defences and escapes, face their anxiety, make suitable choices and take responsibility for their lives.

The risk of confrontation

To find the courage to act individuals need to deal not only with what I call **ego management** issues at Levels 1 and 2 but also the **existential issues** at Level 3 of the iceberg, as illustrated in Figure 4. An iceberg is incredibly stable because 80 per cent of it is below the surface of the waterline. It is this 80 per cent that maintains the status quo in organisations and in ourselves. Traditional change programmes deal only with the 60 per cent at Levels 1 and 2. Without awareness, understanding and incorporation of the other 40 per cent into everyday communications and actions, the probability of change is substantially reduced.

The project manager and sales executive in the example on p. 4 in Chapter 1 lacked the courage to take the risk of speaking their minds even though they had worked at Levels 1 and 2 and acquired the appropriate skills and knowledge. Their behaviour will remain unchanged until they also acquire an approach developed at Level 3 that encourages them to *act despite their fears*.

This approach is one that constantly reminds them that they are responsible for events they previously thought were 'happening to them'. A process that challenges them to look at the price they are paying for the choices they make; increases their sense of freedom through recognition of their own part in their current situation. It highlights their belief that there is almost nothing they can do to change their situation and helps them explore what they *can* do.

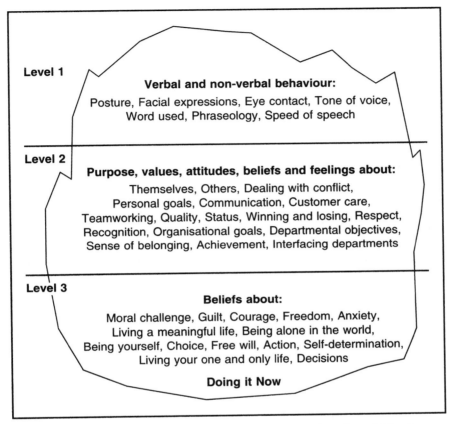

Level 1

Verbal and non-verbal behaviour:

Posture, Facial expressions, Eye contact, Tone of voice,
Word used, Phraseology, Speed of speech

Level 2

Purpose, values, attitudes, beliefs and feelings about:

Themselves, Others, Dealing with conflict,
Personal goals, Communication, Customer care,
Teamworking, Quality, Status, Winning and losing, Respect,
Recognition, Organisational goals, Departmental objectives,
Sense of belonging, Achievement, Interfacing departments

Level 3

Beliefs about:

Moral challenge, Guilt, Courage, Freedom, Anxiety,
Living a meaningful life, Being alone in the world,
Being yourself, Choice, Free will, Action, Self-determination,
Living your one and only life, Decisions

Doing it Now

Figure 4 The 'iceberg' model of change, including the existential level

The courage resulting from the adoption of this existential approach will provide a new confidence to take the actions necessary to confront company politics and depower the saboteurs. Awareness of personal responsibility for every decision made, even the decision not to decide, and the inevitable anxiety associated not only with action but also inaction will ensure long-term change in the culture of the organisation.

3 Why Play Politics and Why Acquiesce?

'Risk is the tariff for leaving the land of predictable misery.'

(*Howard Figler*)

Why play politics, and why acquiesce?

Company politics comes in all shapes and sizes, but whether they're small and incidental or large and strategic they always have an influence on the effectiveness of the organisation. The following are a couple of examples of game-playing that I came across recently which illustrate the ego management that drives the behaviour of both those who play and those who acquiesce to politics:

I was running a workshop in a company recently and asked the receptionist to tell us when the sandwich lady arrived. When we broke for coffee and I asked her if she had arrived, she looked mock horrified and said that she had forgotten to tell us. The way she looked made me feel sure that she had deliberately forgotten. *Why? Why would she do that?*

Late last year I flew to Belfast to help the CEO of a Group of 9 Companies. The CEO, the 9 MDs and 1 Board member from each of the companies had gone to a hotel to write their strategic plan. On their return they couldn't understand why the remaining Board members paid only lip-service to this plan. I said that I suspected they would not have 'bought into' the strategic plan even if those left behind had devised the very same strategy whilst chatting around the coffee machine. *Why? Why would they reject a strategy that they too, in the absence of the rest of their team, came up with?*

The answer to every example of such sabotaging behaviour is the same:

> When people have a choice between a rational decision and their ego, they always choose their ego!

Somehow the receptionist felt badly enough about herself to sabotage us. Instead of doing the rational thing of simply letting us know when the sandwich lady arrived, it made her feel better about herself to sabotage us. Somehow those Board members left behind felt badly enough about themselves to sabotage those lucky enough to be included in the policy-making expedition to the hotel. Sabotaging the others' efforts made them feel better about themselves, whatever the merits of the plan. The *defence of our self-image (our ego) always takes precedence over an objective approach.* This practice of defending our ego is what I call '*ego management*' in contrast with '*rational management*' which is what everyone pretends is going on.

Personal agendas are followed in order to satisfy personal goals which support the ego. Most individuals in a meeting have a personal agenda. If a team are attempting to devise a sales strategy, the sales executive will want to sell as much as he can to get his commission and to hell with whether the customer actually pays. The accountant is interested in steady, safe sales where he can be sure that bad debts are going to be kept to a minimum. The rational thing to do is to work together to devise a sales strategy that will satisfy the organisational goals and make everyone successful, but what happens is that, if you look around the room, everyone is totally concerned about how they feel about themselves and their ego.

As the saboteurs defend their ego, so do those who acquiesce in their behaviour. The rational decision may be to confront the saboteurs' personal agendas, inform management or leave the company but in the defence of their ego they choose to suffer the *consequences of their own inaction.*

It is easy to see how such behaviour can escalate. Subversive retaliation or careful avoidance by those on the receiving end of sabotage results in the expenditure of more energy dealing with the competition inside the organisation than with the competition outside it!

So why don't individuals act? Why do they focus on defending their ego rather than take the risk of saying what they mean and doing what they say?

Fear and ego management

Fear is the answer that springs to mind. There are a number of fears that control our desire to act:

- Fear of looking foolish
- Fear of being disliked
- Fear of standing out
- Fear of being rejected
- Fear of losing
- Fear of being out on a limb
- Fear of getting it wrong
- Fear of being shouted at
- Fear of failure
- Fear of uncertainty.

Have you ever been in a meeting and the more you don't speak the more nervous you feel about hearing the sound of your own voice and the more nervous you become, the more stupid what you have to say sounds in your head? If and when you eventually do pluck up the courage to speak, you either make a hash of it or, because of the delay, it's now out of context and so you do in fact sound stupid! Yet we have no difficulty in saying what we mean as soon as we break for coffee! As soon as the group dynamics change, so do our fears and we feel safe enough to say what we mean. Boy, do we say what we mean!

The disillusionment in organisations is not merely the result of the frustration of having work blocked by saboteurs but also the frustration with yourself for putting up with them. Many suffer the same misgivings in their private lives – living an inauthentic life, unhappy, discontented and unfulfilled, yet confused by their unwillingness to take the risk of change for fear of upsetting others, of getting it wrong or of the unknown.

Why do individuals behave in such an inauthentic manner? Why did the receptionist and the Board members feel the need to defend their egos? Ego management starts very young, caused by parents who tend to think that they're right and so the children learn that the way to win their *approval and recognition* is to conform to their wishes. This is reinforced by teachers, religious instructors, lecturers and so on who likewise reward their students for doing things 'right' in their eyes and punish them for doing things 'wrong'. When they are punished for being 'wrong' they are made to feel stupid and as a consequence begin to lose some of their confidence in expressing their own ideas and perceptions.

By the time individuals enter work they have learned to suppress their own opinions, feelings, experience and creativity and to live by the standards of others in an attempt to win their approval. So strong is this need that even as successful adults individuals still feel put out if their parents fail to acknowledge their status and success. It is in trying to win this approval that people *hide their imperfections* both from themselves and from others. The mechanism used to hide imperfections is ego management – for example, they may say they've done something they haven't rather than admit to a fault.

This need to cover up for the fear of making mistakes and feeling stupid results in

(a) Some people sabotage the system either openly and aggressively or secretly and manipulatively in an attempt to score points. The receptionist lacked self-confidence as she had been brought up in an environment where all relationships were seen in terms of winning and losing. She now feels that if she's not winning she's losing. The only way she feels she can win and therefore feel good is to sabotage others so that they lose and feel bad. The Board members felt publicly humiliated by their apparent demotion and to hide the threat to their self-esteem demonstrated their power by sabotaging the CEO and other Board members.

(b) Others perpetuate the status quo by attempting to do their job in spite of the saboteurs. They say nothing to the saboteurs or management for fear of getting it wrong, being a misfit, making waves, being disliked, losing the chance of promotion, disapproval, the discomfort of an argument and so on. They hide their imperfections by trying to be what they imagine others expect them to be. Superficially, they keep their heads down, do what they are told and suppress their views, ideas and opinions. Yet bubbling underneath and surfacing at every 'safe' opportunity – at the coffee machine, in workshops, in the pub at lunchtime – are the frustrations, anger, stresses, disappointments, feelings of impotence and depression of those who see a better way of doing things yet are too scared to say.

In other words, rather than take the risk of being what they want to be or saying what they want to say, individuals defend their egos in an attempt to win recognition and approval. Some do it through sabotage and some through acquiescing in sabotage.

Catastrophic fantasies

In the economic climate of today some of the pressures not to act authentically are real, but many are imagined:

> I knew a man who could not tell his parents that he wanted to marry a woman of a different religion for fear it would kill them. He lived secretly with this woman, only his friends knowing, and denied them both children, creating great tension until finally, after his mother's death, and when he was well into his 50s he owned up to his father. His father's reaction both stunned and devastated him and his girlfriend; he was thrilled that he had found someone to love and said that his mother would have been thrilled too – all she worried about and prayed for was that her son would find a woman who loved him and could have his children – her grandchildren – for him. What a waste of life . . . All because of some imagined catastrophe.

This is a gross example of what both saboteurs and those who acquiesce in them do. They worry about what others will think, about what might happen if they do or say something that others don't like. In other words, 'catastrophic fantasies' are what stop people being authentic: they stop people acting. Catastrophic fantasies are Catastrophic because we always think the worst ('If I ask for a move I'll get the sack') and are Fantasies because they rarely happen! You won't get the sack for asking for a move.

Individuals spend days weeks, nights worrying when most of the time their worries are unfounded. In the words of Mark Twain:

> 'I have known many great troubles but most of them rarely happened.'

Because of their catastrophic fantasies, people hold themselves back rather than take the risk of being honest. They sit in a meeting silently disagreeing with what's being said only to voice their opinion when they feel safe in a huddle with those they trust during the coffee break. To their surprise, they find that everyone else in their particular huddle didn't agree either, but no one had the nerve to say so.

Yet it is important to remember that on the occasions when we *have* taken the risk and said or done what we believe is right, nothing catastrophic happens. Have you ever been at a meeting when someone is explaining something that everyone else appears to understand and agree with and someone pipes up with, 'I'm sorry but I'm totally confused' or, 'I don't agree with that' and, amazingly, nearly all the others noisily express the same view with a smile of relief?

If individuals in organisations could put aside their need to pretend perfection by using ego-defensive tactics (which fool no-one anyway) and instead choose to be authentic, they could begin to work with each other in a cooperative relationship combining their strengths and compensating for their weaknesses in achieving common goals:

Paul Wilson, senior internal consultant working for a large corporation, felt angry that the Board were to bring in external consultants to train them in what he had already successfully done at their request for the rest of the company. Rather than sabotage or acquiesce in the decision by staying and playing games or doing half a job, he took the risk of confronting the Board, who subsequently agreed to use him. He chose to hold true to his beliefs and act authentically, which created the change that was *better for the organisation as well as for himself.*

Developing an existential approach to long-term change

The problem is that most individuals convince themselves that *they have no choice in life*. Because their world is full of commitments and obligations (husband or wife, children, elderly parent, mortgage, need to eat) they find it difficult to accept that they have this freedom to choose.

To be *existentially aware*, individuals need to accept that they alone block themselves from being themselves and that they are in the situation they find themselves because they have:

- made choices
- freely, and are therefore
- responsible for their life predicament

whereas most people feel that they have:

- no choice but to live their life for everyone else
- feel trapped, and
- blame others for it!

Changing organisation cultures requires individuals to *overcome their ego management issues* and to *live existentially*. Once they know the desired values, attitudes, behaviours, if they are to act them out every minute of every day in pursuit of the vision, mission and objectives each individual has to answer seven questions.

(a)   Who are you trying to please?

Many individuals find it difficult to change because in worrying about what others will think they blame them for their own behaviour. People will say to me: 'I'm miserable as sin, I hate what I'm doing but I can't do anything about it.'

So I ask, 'Why not? Who are you trying to please?' and they reply, 'My boss,' 'The saboteurs,' 'My husband,' 'My wife,' 'My kids.' They feel powerless to do what matters to them and are therefore neither being authentic nor living a meaningful life and so naturally become depressed, stressed and ill.

Why do we try and please everyone but ourselves? As I said earlier, as children, we are encouraged to believe that others know best, especially in our education system and often in our families. We are taught that there is a right and a wrong, and made to look foolish if we do not abide by this perception; the perception of those in *authority*. This results in the suppression of our own view, needs and wants. You must live your life according to *your own values* which define what's right and wrong *for you*.

(b)   Who's pulling your strings?

I tell people that no-one is pulling their strings, they are not puppets, they are in control of their life and more importantly, *responsible for it*.

No one can make you feel anything or do anything. If you choose to conform to other people's needs, wants and values, you have only yourself to blame. The reward for conforming to others demands is peace for you – you have an *'anything for peace'* approach to your life. But is it peaceful? Not in the middle of the night. Not in the long term. To give up your own integrity for the sake of a few minutes', days' or weeks' peace is a huge price to pay for an unfulfilled life.

(c)   What are you waiting for?

I see people week after week who make a decision but don't change; they don't act. They wait and wait until they're dead. I confront people so that they act now.

In the Barry Sonnenfeld-directed film *Get Shorty* (1996), John Travolta makes a very existential point: the female co-star asks in the car after a fight in a hotel, 'Were you scared?' and he says, 'Yes.' So she says, 'You don't look scared' and he says, 'I'm not now, I was then. How long do you want me to feel scared?' He was aware that he could *choose* how long to feel anything. If you want to do something, do it now.

(d)   What's the worst thing that can happen?

People won't do the silliest things in case they get it wrong and they always imagine the worst will happen. So if someone won't ask the person next to them to stop smoking I say, 'What's the worst thing that will happen?' 'Everyone will hate me,' they respond.

(e)   Will it really happen?

'Will that really happen?' I ask. 'No' they reply sheepishly. 'Well what *will* happen?' 'She won't like me for 3 days.' And I ask, 'And then?,' to which they reply grinning, 'And then she'll like me again!' So do it because:

(a) You have no idea if she will or will not be offended until you ask her!
(b) She probably doesn't like you now!
(c) If she doesn't talk to you for three days, so? So what? So she'll talk to you *after* three days!

(f)   How does it feel now, standing still?

If you don't mention it, it's equally stressful isn't it? So stress and anxiety are an *inevitable part of living*, whether you go for what you believe in or deny what you believe in.

People imagine that however bad it is right now, it'll be worse if they try and change. It is worth considering however, that you *know* it's 100 per cent bad now but if you change you have at least a 50 per cent chance that it might be better! If you stand still by always denying your own needs and in order to live according to other people's needs' you are wasting your life.

(g)   What would you do if you knew you only had 6 months left to live?

So instead of waiting to regret an unfulfilled life on your deathbed, do it now. Ask yourself: 'If I am going to die in 6 months' time what would I do with the rest of my life?' Well you wouldn't be worrying about what the person sitting next to you will say or do if you ask them to stop smoking, would you?! You'd just ask them. When you consider the prospect of having a mere 6 months left to live, it helps to put things into perspective, helps to clarify your values and helps you to do what's important to you rather than trying to get it ' right' in other people's eyes.

Rabbi Hillel expresses the existential approach succinctly in the following well known sentences:

> If I am not for myself who will be,
> If I am for myself alone what am I?
> If not now when?

Confronting company politics through existential awareness

If organisations are to work with the explicit contract of culture-change programmes, it will require individuals to understand and acknowledge:

1   Their fear of taking the risk of being themselves and their dependency on ego management
2   Their personal responsibility for their life predicament and the importance of existential awareness.

To live a more authentic life individuals need to overcome certain *existential hurdles* that confront them every day of their lives. These hurdles are the need to:

- Take the risk of being themselves
- Be decisive and act
- Live with uncertainty
- Accept anxiety as part of life
- Drop the illusion of ever being in control
- Stop blaming others, the situation or 'life' itself
- Overcome the illusion of hopelessness and helplessness

By overcoming these hurdles they will find it easier to act, re-evaluate and act again. The *development of an existential approach* will allow them to:

> 1 take *responsibility* for their situation (no blaming others)
> 2 become aware of their own standards and *values* and live according to them (not everyone else's)
> 3 be aware that they always have a *choice* (they are not as 'stuck' as they think they are)
> 4 accept *anxiety* as an inevitable part of being *free* (stop hoping to avoid it)
> 5 be *authentic* (believe that it is OK to be themselves, not what everyone else wants them to be)
> 6 live a *meaningful life* (not one that they will end up regretting)

Well it's either that or stay the same! As Howard Figler puts it:

> *Risk is the tariff for leaving the land of predictable misery.*

4 Taking Action in a Hostile Environment

'... the choice either to participate in the collective psychosis or to take a risk and become healthy and perhaps crucified.'

(*Fritz Perls*)

Creating the ideal environment

Chapter 3 ended with the quote from Howard Figler: 'Risk is the tariff for leaving the land of predictable misery'. Traditionally, organisation development and culture change programmes have used the *humanistic approach* in the attempt to rectify the '*predictable misery*' in organisations by creating a safe and supportive environment. They neglect to emphasise the 'risk'. Existentialists, on the other hand, have a less optimistic view stressing as they do the *difficulty of accepting and exercising the freedom* to act in circumstances where the outcome is uncertain.

Humanists believe that if individuals are allowed to develop freely, without undue constraints, they will become rational, socialised beings. Humanistic psychology took shape in America in the decade after the Second World War when the workplace was undergoing rapid changes. People were being replaced by machines; tasks were becoming narrower and more specialised. As a result, people began to feel alienated from their jobs. Humanists emphasised the role that human beings have in directing their own lives; that they possess an innate capacity for creativity and goodness; that they are guided by purpose and meaning, are capable of responsibility and have an innate motivation to maximise their capabilities and fulfil their potential.

Because humanists are interested in how things or *phenomena* appear to each individual and how they *experience* their worlds and themselves, it is known as a 'phenomenological' or 'experiential approach'. Humanists believe that learning is best when we experience or do something for ourselves and use both our thought process and our feelings, rather than observe someone else or hear about it. This is known as '*experiential learning*', and has taken over most management training where participants become involved in activities which use their past experience, make them aware of current behaviours and try out alternative approaches.

Another important focus is on the individuals' potential for choice. Because of our obligations, fear, apathy, negative outcomes, social constraints, or the belief that we have no alternative we may not make choices, but for humanists, the fact remains that in all situations we have a *choice*. The freedom to choose means that each individual can play a part in the creation of the person they are to become. Thus the best way to encourage self-development is to become aware of your feelings, motivations, wishes and what influences you. This process is termed 'personal growth'.

The humanistic concept of self-actualisation

Carl Rogers and *Abraham Maslow* are the main thinkers in the Humanistic school and both believe that the prime motivation in human life is the drive towards *self-actualisation*, the fulfilment of our capabilities.

According to Rogers (1970), the only way to solve this problem is to create a *client-centred* atmosphere, one which is warm and accepting, perceives the individual's world as he or she does and, most importantly, offers respect and approval with no conditions, which he terms 'unconditional positive regard'. In this accepting atmosphere, the individual can confront feelings and experiences that are inconsistent with the self and thereby broaden the self to include the total experience of the organism. Thus freed, the individual is brought back into congruence and can once again proceed with self-actualisation.

Like Rogers, Maslow (1954) started out with the premise that human beings are basically good and that all their behaviour issues from a single master motive, the drive toward self-actualisation defined as 'an ongoing actualisation of potential, capacities and talents' (cited in 'Psycho-sources', 1973, p. 140). Maslow's contribution to the humanistic approach was his concept of the *hierarchy of needs*, a series of needs that must be met in the process of development before the adult can begin to pursue self-actualisation. The first level is Physiological needs, such as food and water, the next level is Safety from danger such as fire, cold and financial disaster; the third level is a Sense of Belonging, which includes love and friendship; next comes the need for Self-esteem such as status, recognition and respect. Only when these are satisfied is the final level of

Self-actualisation reached which includes competence, achievement and meaningfulness.

Maslow argued that unless basic needs are met higher ones cannot be satisfied. People are motivated to reach the top of the hierarchy, but may stop for fear of losing what they have or because they imagine they are blocked by external social forces. Those who do not reach self-actualisation may experience feelings of non-fulfilment. An individual may have a job, take care of their children and to all intents and purposes function in an effective manner, yet still feel lonely, alienated and ineffectual. Maslow called this state 'the psychopathology of the normal'. Human beings, Maslow argued, require a great deal more than mere 'adjustment' and psychology should be concerned with helping people live fulfilled, rich and creative lives. Rogers' and Maslow's unremitting optimism regarding the drive to self-actualisation and the preoccupation with self-fulfilment is typical of humanistic psychology.

The humanistic model, emphasising as it does the self-concept, the uniqueness of the individual, the importance of values and meaning and our potential for self-direction and personal growth, has had a major and increasing influence upon contemporary thought and management theory.

The humanistic approach in practice

Culture-change consultants, either wittingly or unwittingly, use this humanistic approach. The following case study illustrates the importance of a supportive climate for the development of potential. Yet issues of dependence and counterdependence on authority and the lack of courage to take personal responsibility for their own actions, neither of which were dealt with in the humanistic approach, meant that the employees could not sustain the changes.

Harlow Systems, a software house, had grown rapidly from its inception in 1985 both in terms of market penetration and revenue. Most of the original staff were occupying management positions but the initial feelings of energy, commitment and customer care had gone, revenue growth had levelled off, margins had declined and the management was turning inward looking to understand what had gone wrong. The focus of the business therefore was no longer on success but on seeking to explain, justify or excuse failure.

As a result most individuals throughout the entire company were:

- Keeping their heads down
- Having corridor meetings
- Doing the minimum
- Hiding behind procedures to avoid responsibility for their actions or inaction
- Using 'rocking horse management' – lots of movement but never getting anywhere
- Circumventing management attempts to measure or control
- Taking time out from their working day
- Inflating future sales projections
- Underestimating costs or time to complete projects
- Withholding information
- Using systems inconsistently or not at all
- Deliberately accentuating departmental differences (e.g. 'pedestrian' versus 'cavalier', as we saw in Chapter 1).

Organisational issues

The MD and his management team tried to rectify the situation using all the conventional remedies for addressing organisational issues such as:

- Reorganisation by geography and vertical market sector
- Restructuring from a functional to a matrix organisation
- Extensive product training
- New and improved compensation and benefits
- Weeding out failures (some real and some perceived)
- Redefinition of job function and personnel descriptions
- Introduction of departmental budgets
- Increased measurement and control of results
- Increased budgetary control and measurement against target
- Quarterly, then monthly, staff reviews.

Whilst all the changes were welcomed at first by management and perceived to be a step in the right direction, any benefit was short term. There was no actual longer-term benefit that had any impact on revenue or profit.

These processes took a number of years to be considered, tried and found wanting. In the meantime, the business was getting progressively weaker and the management team less effective, partially through exhaustion and partially through frustration with each other and the lack of success. This resulted in even more energy turned inward in an attempt to resolve organisational issues rather than energy turned outward in customer care and gaining business.

It was a classic downward spiral of failure.

The significance of process issues

At this point the MD, recognising nothing was working, invited management consultants to look at the business and recommend an action plan to get the company back on track.

After a survey and two top team residential workshops it emerged that the reason people were feeling and behaving as they did was not because of organisational issues but because of *process issues* such as:

- Low morale
- Internal competition
- Mistrust
- Lack of communication
- Top management non-cooperation
- Interdepartmental conflict
- Inaccessibility of the MD
- Lack of strong, cohesive leadership
- No clear vision, mission or objectives
- No shared values, attitudes and behaviours
- Feelings of powerlessness
- Fear of reprisals for autonomous action.

Action for culture change

The consultants recommended the 'humanistic approach' to culture change. It was explained that in the change process the primary responsibility rested upon Harlow themselves. The consultant would play a relatively passive role, since he assumed that Harlow was inherently able to solve its own problems. Approaching Harlow with as few preconceived notions as possible, the consultant worked with the information given by the company, repeating or reflecting back their ideas and helping them to clarify them, and avoiding interpretation of what Harlow was saying or attempting to provide solutions.

This focus was on individual responsibility, autonomy, the facilitative rather than autocratic leadership style, the belief that given the right environment everyone would self-actualise to the good of each other and the company. The creation of a warm and accepting climate by the consultants with the top team was to be mirrored throughout the company. This led to an agreement to put in place a culture change programme and the consultants designed a *TQM programme* to address these process issues.

The management team greeted this idea in a fairly typical manner. Some said 'yes' when they meant 'no', some were openly cynical and others really wanted to change.

The change programme – the humanistic approach

The *creation of the environment* focused on helping people to trust the management and each other through honest, open discussion of significant problems. This should result in development of both self-confidence and confidence in each other such that everyone would feel safe to use their creative potential to make suggestions and come up with mutually acceptable solutions.

As a result the *objective of all meetings* during the change programme was always twofold:

(a)   to address organisational issues
(b)   to address process issues.

The client-centred approach

The consultants used the 'client-centred' approach which followed an orderly and predictable sequence:

1.   Creation of developmental relationships
2.   Expression of feelings and thoughts which had formerly been denied or distorted, including many negative feelings
3.   Self-insight and increased understanding of human relationships, group working and intergroup conflict
4.   The resolution of conflicts and more positive feelings about self and others
5.   Arrival at a point where there is no longer need for the support of the consultants.

The consultants:

• Modelled the appropriate *leadership (facilitator) skills*
• *Trained the managers* in these leadership skills
• Trained appropriate members of staff in *group facilitation skills* for future meetings.

During the 9 months of the change programme, this was to all intents and purposes a highly successful exercise. Other consultants who came in later to work in the company commented on the quality and depth of the work done by the management consultants and the risks they had taken in terms of confronting process issues and creating a humanistic culture. For some time, the humanistic approach resulted in an atmosphere where everyone felt safe, trusted each other and felt good about the company and its future. Yet, the momentum was not sustained. Something was missing.

The management and staff passed each other by

While the management was attempting to internalise the new values, the consultants were carrying the responsibility for leading the company in the humanistic style of working. They inspired the staff, who trusted them and believed that this time the company culture would really change. The consultants encouraged the staff to acquire *follower skills* by understanding the fears and insecurities of the leaders and being more approachable and less critical of them. At the same time, the consultants worked with the *leader's skills* and similarly asked the managers to be sensitive to the fears of their followers, more approachable and less critical.

The followers quickly got the point. They were spending hours with the consultants who were creating a humanistic environment in workshops where they felt safe enough to begin to be honest, creative and 'self-actualise'. In the environment of the workplace, however, they were waiting for the managers to do the same. Since the managers spent less and less time with the consultants as the programme went on, it took them a lot longer to get the point. After 2–3 months, they were finally convinced by the new follower skills of their staff, which gave them the confidence to change.

During this period sabotage, though less obvious, was still bubbling under the surface. Because the management had not clamped down on it with the same conviction as the consultants, the saboteurs were still getting away with it and as time went by therefore their power was reinforced. So after 3 months, as the managers were doing a U-turn to join the rest of the company who were following the consultants, the rest of the company, seeing saboteurs continue to get away with their strangle hold on the culture, were doing a U-turn back to square one!

An example of this was Harry Lloyd, the Support Director, who took some time to be convinced that the programme was worthwhile until his staff took the time to discuss their problems and inform him of their progress. However, the moment he actively began to participate in workshops, projects and surveys, some of his staff remained resentful about his prior indifference towards them and the broken promises during the first couple of months.

Nevertheless, morale remained high whilst the management consultants were facilitating all meetings. Even though most individuals in the organisation at the beginning of the change programme were sceptical about the focus on process issues and facilitation, within 3 months everyone agreed that process issues were key to the achievement of their best first quarter sales performance ever.

The momentum was unsustained

It started to disintegrate during the second quarter when the saboteurs appeared to be exempt from the new rules of behaviour and competition began to resurface. These bids for power and control were most noticeable amongst the management team. Certain managers were frightened to maintain a culture where staff were free to experiment with new behaviour and ideas since mistakes would reflect on them. Consequently, they began to reintroduce old habits of 'command and control' and to drive their personal agendas through Quality meetings.

Because of this, individuals found it hard to maintain the atmosphere when left to their own devices. They found it impossible to take risks when left alone with colleagues or managers who had a reputation for making others look small. They feared either being publicly humiliated during meetings or privately undermined by the selective dissemination of half-truths. Tom Williams, a Sales Support Consultant, who was trained in facilitating skills, had no formal authority and could not gain sufficient respect from managers on Quality project teams. Alan Bostock, the Sales Director, would shut out any attempt at intervention, professing support for the programme yet pleading he had to 'get the *real* work done'. Thus the saboteurs were able to re-establish their hold over the company culture the moment that the consultants left some 9 months after the change programme began.

Even when some individuals gave up the gross manifestations of external control they still maintained it subtly, some even unaware that they were doing so. During a meeting with an internal facilitator, they would agree a contract and let the facilitator process the meeting until, towards the end, when their time was limited they would autocratically shut down the conversation and make a decision!

For example, Jerry Chandler, the MD, would schedule an hour for a meeting before he had to catch a flight for Paris. He would leave the meeting by saying, 'Sorry guys I have to catch a plane'. In doing so he had recreated the 'old culture' and destroyed any goodwill that had been developed. This left everyone feeling confused, angry and resigned to the fact that nothing ever changes and that they themselves were powerless.

The problem is that most managers work out of the Organisational issues paradigm rather than a Process issues one. In the early days of a change programme, process-based meetings take hours as the staff learn to be open and honest, though eventually the meetings become shorter.

The humanistic approach had provided everyone with the skills. They had an opportunity in a safe environment to become aware of and begin to deal with their ego management issues. They developed teambuilding skills and understood the importance the facilitation of the group dynamics, yet their lack of an existential approach made them sit and wait until confronting the politics was either made easy in a workshop environment or done by someone else.

The change programme – the existential approach

Tom Williams stopped himself from acting because of his fantasies about the bad things that would happen if he dared be himself. He chose to say nothing, go along with the sabotage of the programme, remain unhappy at work and blend in rather than stick his neck out and be authentic:

> the choice either to participate in the collective psychosis or to take a risk and become healthy and perhaps crucified.
>
> (*Perls*, 1971, p. 32)

Just as Harry Lloyd did at the beginning of the programme, rather than take the risk of looking stupid or being disliked (being 'crucified') by being authentic (being 'healthy') he preferred to keep his head down and stay with what he imagined was going to remain the 'collective psychosis' of the company culture.

The humanistic approach had led both Tom and Harry to believe that a safe and supportive climate is a crucial element of change. Humanistic consultants advocate giving employees the freedom to make autonomous choices as a means of motivating them to use their potential in the pursuit of self-actualisation. In other words, the assumption is that if you give people freedom they'll take it. But they don't in a *hostile environment*. While the humanists assume that a person will *automatically* use their freedom to develop their potential, the existentialists less optimistically stress the difficulty of *accepting* and *exercising freedom*.

As Jerry Chandler packed up to leave, no one spoke out. It was up to the rest of the group – the majority! – to stick their neck out and say 'NO! If that's the case we'll meet again'. It would have been better for everyone, including Jerry, to wait until they had a consensus that everyone was committed to rather than a so-called 'decision' that the minority had made. When it's a minority decision, people will sabotage it. We're back to a downward spiral of sabotage.

The existential approach – the moral challenge

Whereas the humanists speak of self-actualisation, the existentialists speak of the anguish of both exercising freedom and the self-confrontation when we avoid it. Existentialists take the pragmatic view that whilst it would be nice to have a safe environment, since most leaders are unlikely to sack the one-third who are saboteurs or find the time to put the effort into zero tolerance, each individual is left to behave authentically and act in a *hostile* environment. An existentialist would see change as the following:

Life is inherently unjust, and although the support of others can be very helpful we are ultimately alone, must make our own decisions, act and deal with the consequences.

Existentialists regard freedom as less as a gift than as a *moral challenge*. Existentialists emphasise the *active* rather than the *passive* aspects of becoming your own person and urge each individual to clarify their personal values. Existentialists encourage individuals to take responsibility for their situation because they have chosen it, and to show them that they are free – indeed *obligated* – to choose better ways of dealing with it.

Existentialism is also based on the phenomenological approach. Like the humanists, existentialists try to see the client's world from his or her perspective but the tone is very different. Existentialists create a less warm and comfortable environment than the humanists, and are more *confrontational*. They see change as a sort of *heroic partnership* – consultant and client together – facing a world where personal values are hard to find and harder still to act upon. In this way the consultants consistently confront their clients with their responsibility for their own lives by surfacing the illogical fears and images that prevent their action.

The existential model has its origins in philosophy and literature and stems from the writings of European philosophers such as Heideggar, Kierkegaard and Sartre. Like humanism, existentialism was a response to dehumanisation, but on a larger scale. Existentialists are concerned with the social predicament of the individual caused by the rise of industrialisation, the breakdown of traditional faith and the depersonalisation of the individual in a standardised mass culture. This loss of meaning and values in human existence, termed 'alienation', is seen as a kind of spiritual death and in the attempt to regain purpose and meaning, existential psychology has grown in popularity during the last three decades through the work of such people as the America psychologists, Rollo May and Victor Frankl, and the British psychiatrist, R.D. Laing.

Whereas humanists seek to brighten the picture, existentialists elucidate the problem, and claim that the human condition is by nature one of uncertainty and anxiety. This may seem depressing but the existentialists hold out the hope of a highly meaningful life. With no surviving systems of received truth, it becomes the responsibility of every individual to shape their own identity and to make their existence meaningful – to make their life count for something – not by following external rules offered by philosophy, religion or science but by *taking risks*, doing *what feels right* and *learning and developing* from each experience.

(a)   Existence precedes essence

A fundamental concept in existentialism is that while our *existence* is a given our *essence*, what we make of our existence, is up to us:

• The youth who defiantly blurts out 'Well, I didn't ask to be born' is stating a profound truth. But it is irrelevant. For whether he asked to be born or not, here he is in the world and answerable for one human life – his own.• (*Coleman and Hammen*, 1974, p. 35)

Once we exist, what we make of ourselves, our essence, is up to us. Existence precedes essence.

(b)   Responsibility, freedom and choice

The essence of a person who creates his own essence is an open question. First man *is* and then he must ask himself *what* he is. In this way, man is responsible for giving meaning to his existence, in the process of living his own life. Responsibility viewed in this manner is inseparably linked to *freedom* – the freedom to *choose*. However, most individuals do not exercise this freedom to choose because their need for recognition has lead them to believe that they must live their life according to certain values: those of the organisation, the family, the church or society.

Existentialists believe that this locus of values has been misplaced. It does, in fact, rest with ourselves. No matter from which higher authority we choose to get advice on how to live our life, we have already made up our minds what advice we want by the mere act of choosing our adviser. Even when we choose our adviser as objectively as possible, we still decide *after* the advice is given whether or not to follow it. We are left with the inescapable conclusion that *we make our own advice*!

Every day we choose what we are going to do or not do, say or not say, what goals we will pursue or forgo, who we will put first or last, what we will continue with or what we will change. Since to choose is by definition an act of valuing one thing over another, it is in the very act of choosing that we point to those *values* by which we wish to live our life. As Sartre put it: 'I am my choices.'

The difficulty is that we never know whether this or that choice is the one we should have made because there are no 'advisers' out there to justify our choices other than the ones we choose ourselves. We are ultimately the author of all our choices and can turn to no authority to justify them.

Because finding satisfying values and living by them is a lonely and highly individual matter, Sartre, in plays such as *No Exit* (1955), saw man's freedom as a curse: 'Man is condemned to be free.' He saw man's freedom to shape his own essence as 'both his agony and his glory':

> • Since we are inescapably the architects of our own life, each person must have the courage to break away from old patterns, stand alone and find their own meaning. •

Morris (1966, p. 135) has stated the existential position in three clear propositions:

> 1. 'I am a *choosing* agent unable to avoid choosing my way through life.'
> 2. 'I am a *free* agent, absolutely free to set the goals of my own life.'
> 3. 'I am a *responsible* agent, personally accountable for my free choices as they are revealed in how I live my life.'

In choosing what he is to become, the individual is seen as having absolute freedom: even *refusing to choose* represents a choice.

(c)   Authorship of our own values

There appears to be 'no exit' from this overpowering responsibility (Sartre, 1955) for if there were a universal law which we all had to automatically obey, if we knew what was right and wrong, humane and inhumane, we could no longer call ourselves *free*. We could not choose, but would merely be acting out the destiny of man, speaking lines in a vast theatre play which had been written in advance of our utterance. All we would have to do is act it out. So everyone creates values by choosing; the difficulty for individuals is accepting responsibility for the authorship of one's own values.

Many of us cannot stand the thought of living a life which is an open-ended question. We do not want our essence to be left up to us. We want someone to advise us on how to act, how to be, what we believe. But blind conformity to the group leads to a wasted life for which the individual cannot blame any one else. Our lack of essence, our 'nothingness', should not be seen as a deformity to be corrected by others but rather as a challenge to make something worthwhile of our life.

(d)   Life must have meaning

Sartre believed that a central human characteristic is that our life must have meaning and that, since there is no innate meaning to life, this is a highly individual matter. However, he also believed that we all have an obligation to learn to *live constructively* with ourselves, and with others. The most important consideration is not what we can *get out* of life, but what we can *put into* it. Our life can be fulfilling only if it involves socially constructive values and choices. Hence, there will be commonality in the values chosen by different individuals who are trying to live authentically.

Comparison of humanistic and existential approaches

The fundamental differences between the humanistic and existential approaches are outlined in Table 2.

Table 2 The humanistic and existential approach

Humanism/ego management	*Existentialism/existential issues*
The view of humans is *positive*: humans have an innate inclination to become fully functioning, actualise potential and increase self-awareness, spontaneity, trust in self and inner directedness, given the right conditions	Central focus is on the nature of the *human condition*: the capacity for self-awareness, freedom of choice to decide their fate, responsibility, anxiety, the search for meaning in a meaningless world, being alone in relation to others and death
Focus is on the *present moment* and on experiencing and expressing feelings	Focus is on the *present* and also on the *future* in terms of the choices the individual can take to influence what he is to become
Goal is to provide a safe climate conducive to *self-exploration* so as to recognise blocks to growth, experience aspects of self formerly denied or distorted, move toward openness, have greater trust in themselves and increase spontaneity and aliveness	Goal is to help people see that they are *free*, challenge them to recognise that they are *responsible* for events that they previously thought were happening to them, become aware of their possibilities and identify how they block their own freedom
Each individual is responsible only to himself, but it is assumed that since people are innately good they will not harm others in the process of their *self-actualisation*	Aims to develop individuals' spiritual lives, a process that includes their realising their responsibility to others and to fulfil the vision of human life that you can be anything you choose to *be*; do anything you choose to *do*
The approach is unremittingly *optimistic*, stressing the role of self-actualisation, freedom, potential, and the clear possibility of self-fulfilment	Emphasises the search for authenticity, the struggle to *establish and act on values* Does not hold out any hope for total self-fulfilment; instead, emphasises the sorrows built into life such as the threats to freedom, the anguish of choice, the problem of anxiety and the terror of death
	Sees freedom as a struggle since freedom necessitates responsibility as life expects something from *us* and fulfilment of this responsibility does not guarantee self-actualisation; rather, the reward of accepting responsibility is a kind of peace treaty with the human condition so that individuals can rescue their dignity as human beings
Sees *developmental relationships* as ones where the communication of acceptance, genuineness, warmth unconditional positive regard, respect empathy and permissiveness are stressed	Sees developmental relationships as both supportive and confrontational – a *heroic partnership* facing a world where personally meaningful values are hard to find and even harder to act upon

Table 2 continued overleaf

Table 2 continued

Humanism/ego management	Existentialism/existential issues
Basic techniques include *attentive and active listening*, reflection of content, paraphrasing of feelings, clarification and 'being there' authentically and non-judgementally for the client	Basic techniques include *direct confrontation* to call attention to discrepancies; evaluate the choices they are presently making and encourage them to change
Has wide applicability to individual and groups opening up feelings and getting individuals in contact with their present experience.	Useful for clients with existential concerns such as making choices, dealing with freedom and responsibility, coping with guilt and anxiety, making sense of life and finding values; can be applied both to individuals and groups.

The existential approach to maintaining momentum

The humanistic approach creates a climate where individuals are encouraged to satisfy the personal goal of self-actualisation through the use of their energy and potential in the pursuit and achievement of organisational goals. Yet, the difficulty in maintaining the climate and the risks and discomfort involved in such a pursuit should never be underestimated. Neither should anyone hold out any hope of avoiding them if they are to succeed in living an authentic and meaningful life.

For existentialists each individual has to stand up for their principles every minute of every day, no matter what the cost. Excellent companies have leaders who pursue their vision relentlessly, no matter what the cost to their own popularity. They have zero tolerance of sabotage. Yet, since some leaders are also saboteurs, individuals cannot postpone pursuing their work authentically while waiting for an existential leadership style. Therefore the adoption of an existential approach by each individual who wishes to pursue their values and attitudes which match the desired norms, despite those who don't, is a prerequisite for long-term organisational change.

5 Am I an Existentialist?

'One is also entirely responsible for one's life, not only for one's actions but for one's *failures* to act.' (*Irving Yalom*)

Am I an existentialist?

To achieve organisational objectives despite the obstacles created by saboteurs, individuals must find the courage to break away from their old defences and escapes and be themselves (i.e. be existential). But, we could at this point ask:

> If we are all condemned to creating our own essence, surely we are all unknowing existentialists?

The answer is:

> You cannot be an *unknowing* existentialist.

Every minute of every day we're in situations where we could say one thing and not another, do one thing and not another. But to be an existentialist we must be *aware* of these alternative responses *and* the act of *considering* them. Only then is a genuine choice possible. It is in consciously making a choice that we become aware of our own freedom. It's this conscious awareness of our freedom to choose everything we say or do at every moment of our lives which defines who can and who cannot claim to be an existentialist:

> We differ not in the degree to which we are essenceless, but in the degree to which we respond to it authentically.

On occasions, we have flashes of our freedom. While driving up the motorway on a sunny afternoon, listening to an uplifting piece of music. For one brief existential moment we feel we could do anything with our lives and resolve to change, but by the time we've parked the car the everyday 'reality' that we have created for ourselves crashes back in and we become swamped once more by the events of our life. We return to actualising a concept of what we *should* be, rather than to actualising *ourselves*:

> *This difference between *self*-actualising and self-*image* actualising is *very* important. Most people only live for their image. Where some people have a self, most people have a void, because they are so busy projecting themselves as this or that. This is again the curse of the ideal. The curse that you should not be what you are.*
>
> *(Perls, 1971, p. 20)*

A main concern of existentialists is that, by living constantly under the pressure of other people's expectations, individuals tend to deny thoughts and feelings that are 'unacceptable' to others such as managers, colleagues, saboteurs, parents, friends, and society. Eventually this results in a false outer self which covers a denied authentic inner self.

To avoid this split, people must constantly strive to live 'authentically' – to be aware of their own thoughts and feelings and feel free to express them. This does not mean acting on every impulse. It simply means acknowledging and accepting their feelings and thoughts, no matter how unacceptable they may be to others. Only then can they make meaningful choices and use their creative potential.

So who is authentic?

> *The individual who is free and who knows it. Who knows that every deed and word is a choice, and hence an act of value creation and who knows that he is author of his own life and must be held personally responsible . . . and that these values cannot be justified by conforming to something or somebody outside himself.*
>
> *(Morris, 1966, p. 48)*

To live authentically takes tremendous courage. Most of us are numb to our freedom to be authentic because of our fear of disapproval, of rejection or of looking stupid. Because of these fears, we self-image actualise using ego management. Traditional programmes of change raise the awareness of this and develop alternative modes of behaviour. Yet many still don't take the risk of practising the new behaviours.

Even after learning Level 1 and 2 skills during the Harlow Systems programme, rather than be true to their own values and be different, disagree, confront or act autonomously each individual justified their behaviour 'by conforming to something or somebody outside himself' such as 'the norm', obligations, authority, friendship, rules, procedures, managers and colleagues. They even pointed to the saboteurs like Tom Williams, Harry Lloyd and Jerry Chandler who made autocratic decisions to reverse the new culture. Apparently even a tyrant is better than no leader at all as Erich Fromm puts it in (1941) *Escape From Freedom*.

By consenting to the *values of saboteurs*, they adopted them for themselves and their own lives. That is not to say that those who consent to the norm and accepted convention cannot be existential but that they must take personal responsibility for living their lives in this manner. Existential awareness isn't necessarily about change of circumstance. It can also be about a change of attitude. To know you are free and have chosen means that you can continue to live the life you already live with far less tension:

> ⁶ Before he is enlightened, a man gets up each morning to spend the day tending his fields, returns home to eat his supper, goes to bed, makes love to his woman, and falls asleep. But once he has attained enlightenment, then a man gets up each morning to spend the day tending his fields, returns home to eat his supper, goes to bed, makes love to his woman and falls asleep.⁹ (*Kopp, 1972, p. 139*)

Awareness of our freedom to choose makes us feel powerful. We need no longer use our mental energy in negative thoughts about our life predicament. It may be that to the outsider you have not changed, but to you everything looks and feels different – now you are in control whereas previously you felt others were controlling you.

If, on the other hand, we are not *aware of consenting* to the values of others or we are not aware that we are *free not to consent*, then we are being inauthentic.

Existential model of change

Acting in spite of the risk of being liked or disliked, made to feel clever or stupid, belonging to the team or isolated and out on a limb means living with the *uncertainty of unknown outcomes.* In the attempt to avoid the anxiety associated with risk of the uncertainty of change, individuals instead choose to acquiesce, not to practice the new skills and to stand still in life. They block themselves from change. Yet in reality, this is equally stressful.

It is the recognition that either choice creates anxiety, but that one involves living authentically and the other inauthentically, which is the existential insight at Level 3 that can kick start an individual's process of change. Taking the risk of practising the new self-actualising behaviours in spite of what people think rather than self-image actualising is the existential approach.

Figure 5 is a model of change. Someone who's doing something that he's not happy about may drive home *reflecting* on it, lie in bed *planning* to do things differently and, finally, *experiments* with the new plan.

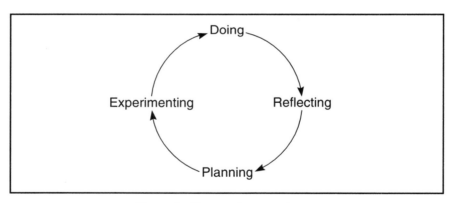

Figure 5   How we learn to change

For example, while chairing a meeting a manager may have handled some conflict badly. He drives home thinking about it, lies in bed and plans a better way of handling it next time and experiments with this plan during the following Monday morning meeting. Organisationally, the manufacture of hand-made widgets may no longer be profitable. The Board reflect on it, plan to automate or manufacture a different product and then experiment with the new plan. This is how individuals and organisations change.

But this is not enough. Individuals and organisations will always have room for improvement. So, the ideal existence is to be continually going around the cycle in an upward spiral, as shown in Figure 6. Always learning, always changing, always improving but never quite getting there since there is no end to development. No individual or organisation can afford to look at itself in the mirror and say:

> ❛Today I am perfect – I never want to be any different than I am today. I never need to change.❜

> Life is a journey of ever decreasing circles, always changing but never quite getting there.

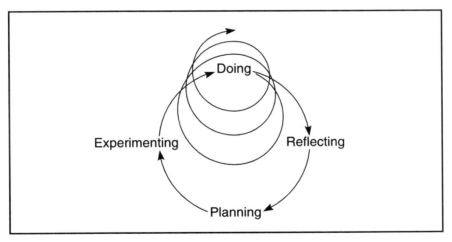

Figure 6   The upward spiral of continuous improvement

If you don't change, the world will change you. Those in the recently privatised public utilities and the civil service, who believed that keeping their heads down, doing the same things, avoiding risks and refusing to change would allow them to hold onto the job security that they originally sought from such an organisation, have found that they were sadly wrong.

If a company's employees don't keep changing in the attempt to continuously improve, another's will. Eventually the first company's commercial existence will be threatened, as was the case with IBM, Russia, and TWA. Every time an organisation is doing things successfully, it must throw away the security of familiarity in an attempt to do even better:

> Security is like happiness, you only get it if you give it away.

The concept of continuous improvement is easy if things are going badly, but it takes guts to keep changing in the quest for continuous improvement when things are going well. Yet this is what successful entrepreneurs and organisations do instinctively: they see change as inevitable and so it holds no fear for them.

If it is easy for entrepreneurs, why isn't everyone open to change and development? It's easy to understand why those who don't see the necessity to change don't change. It's easy to understand why those who are happy with their current situation don't change. But it's not easy to understand why those who aren't happy with their present situation are still not happy to act and change

Looking at Figure 7 and using the example of someone not confronting an issue with a saboteur at a meeting, how would he stop himself from acting?

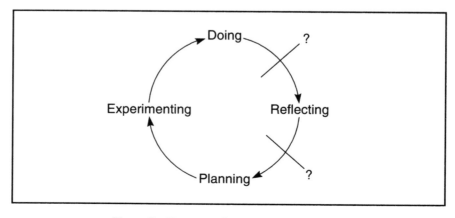

Figure 7   How we sabotage our own change

What sort of things would he be saying to himself to stop himself moving from the Doing to the Reflecting stage? Something like: 'He's a fool anyway,' 'I wasn't feeling well,' 'It's a difficult group,' 'I'm usually very good at this,' 'I've got more important things to worry about'.

What would he say to stop himself moving from Reflecting to Planning?: 'I haven't got the time,' 'I'm too old to change,' 'It's his fault,' 'I'm too tired,' 'I'll do it later,' 'It wasn't that bad'.

These are all examples of the *ego defence mechanisms* used to hide imperfections in order to avoid making mistakes and then feeling stupid, being disapproved of and not getting recognition. Examples of ego defence mechanisms are: 'I wasn't feeling well' (Rationalisation), 'It's his fault' (Blaming) 'It wasn't that bad' (Denial).

So at this point it's an **ego management issue that blocks action**.

In fact, most people spend an enormous amount of time doing the same things, reflecting on them and planning to do something else. They spend weeks, months, even years going around the triangle shown in Figure 8. They think about leaving their partner, plan to do it, but don't: They think about asking for promotion, plan to do it, but don't. They think about asking the person at the next desk to stop smoking, plan to do it, but don't. They think about selling the house and sailing around the world, plan to do it, but don't. They think about starting their own business, plan to do it, but don't. They think about writing the book, plan to do it, but don't. They think about confronting an obstructive, devious character in the organisation or telling their manager about it, plan to do it, but don't. They never act. They never *cross the Rubicon*. Why not? They avoid crossing Rubicons because of *catastrophic fantasies*.

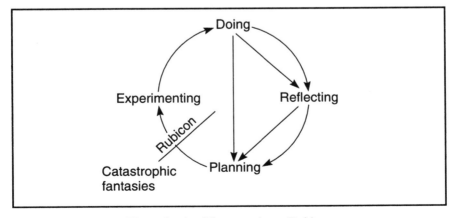

Figure 8   Avoiding crossing a Rubicon

Choosing between existential anxiety and existential guilt

How does it feel crossing Rubicons? How does the thought of asking for a rise or promotion, starting the business, leaving the spouse, changing jobs, selling up and buying the boat feel? It feels *risky* and *scary*. It is fear that stops us crossing Rubicons. Fear of what?

- Fear of the unknown
- Fear of ambiguity
- Fear of uncertainty.

Individuals fear uncertainty because they don't know whether they'll succeed or fail, look foolish or clever, be praised or punished. What do individuals say to themselves to stop themselves experimenting with their idea? Maybe things like: 'What if I fail,' 'What if I hate it?,' 'It could be worse,' 'People might not like it,' 'It's not so bad now,' 'I'll look a fool.'

Crossing Rubicons is stressful, but how does it feel standing still in life? How does life feel right now not taking the risks, keeping your head down, playing it safe, doing the same things and feeling miserable or dissatisfied? Yes – stressful!

At this point it is an **existential issue that stops individuals crossing Rubicons**. They imagine that, by standing still, they can avoid anxiety.

Yet we have two choices in life:

---

1   To suffer the *existential guilt* (and hence stress) of standing still, keeping your head down and playing safe, knowing that you are not fulfilling your life or ambitions, only to look back in later life and regret your lost opportunities. You are now and will always suffer the stress associated with the guilt of looking back on a wasted life and saying 'If only I had . . .'

2   To suffer the *existential anxiety* (and hence stress) of continually trying out new things and fulfilling your life's potential whilst living with the anxiety associated with the uncertainty of taking risks.

As Sartre (1955) said in his play, there is 'no exit' in life but to experience either the Guilt of standing still, or the Anxiety of fulfilling your life's potential. Both are stressful but if we don't want to waste our life, in effect there is no choice.

To paraphrase what George Bernard Shaw said: 'When you are lying on your death bed looking back on your life it's not the things that you did that you'll regret, it's the things you didn't do.' You won't be lying and cringing about how you behaved at a dinner party in 1997, but asking yourself: 'why didn't I ask for promotion', 'why didn't I start my own business', 'why didn't I confront the saboteurs', 'why didn't I sail around the world', 'why didn't I fight for what I believed in?' In the whole scheme of things are the little things that stress you now really so difficult to confront and overcome?

Looking back on your deathbed at, say, 84, the idea of asking the person in another department to stop being obstructive will seem a trivial Rubicon to cross. By not taking the risk, you are responsible for not being everything you could have been and could be.

The humanist's approach to dealing with this inevitable anxiety of crossing Rubicons and experimenting with new behaviour is to create a safe environment. But no matter how hard people try to make the climate safe and supportive it doesn't work. The fact is that confronting the MD, the Sales Director, your immediate manager, who controls your future in the organisation, or a colleague, who could sabotage your career, is very risky because each of them has their own ego management issues and existential fears that might lead them to respond negatively. This is the catastrophic fantasy we all carry with us (and it could be real). The message from the existential model of 'Crossing Rubicons' is that change is dangerous because of the inevitable anxiety created by the uncertainty of outcomes. Therefore a change programme has to focus on **danger and action, not safety and action**.

Had this lesson of the Rubicon been given to the Harlow Systems management team at the beginning of the change programme, they would have been prepared to live with the anxiety of stepping out of their office sooner. They were waiting for it to be safe. Had the followers understood how their anxieties about sticking their neck out – had helped create the low morale in the first place, they would have been less dependent on the consultants and subsequently the management for taking the lead. They were also waiting for it to be safe.

Action would have created a new dynamic in the organisation: failure to act lead back to the status quo of untapped potential and energy.

Wasting our life by playing safe

Franz Kafka's novel *The Trial* (1925) is all about our 'delusion' that we are not guilty of living an unlived life. The following parable, related near the end of the book (pp. 235–7), says it all:

•Before the Law stands a doorkeeper on guard. To this door-keeper there comes a man from the country who begs for admittance to the Law. But the doorkeeper says that he cannot admit the man at the moment. The man, on reflection, asks if he will be allowed, then, to enter later. 'It is possible,' answers the door-keeper, 'but not at this moment.' Since the door leading into the Law stands open as usual and the door-keeper steps to one side, the man bends down to peer through the entrance. When the door-keeper sees that, he laughs and says: 'If you are so strongly tempted, try to get in without my permission. But note that I am powerful. And I am only the lowest door-keeper. From hall to hall, keepers stand at every door, one more powerful than the other. Even the third of these has an aspect that even I cannot bear to look at.' These are difficulties which the man from the country has not expected to meet, the Law, he thinks, should be accessible to every man and at all times, and when he looks more closely at the door-keeper in his furred robe, with his huge pointed nose and long thin, Tartar beard, he decides that he had better wait until he gets permission to enter. The door-keeper gives him a stool and lets him sit down at the side of the door. There he sits waiting for days and years. He makes many attempts to be allowed in and wearies the door-keeper with his importunity. The door-keeper often engages him in brief conversation, asking him about his home and about other matters, but the questions are put quite impersonally, as great men put questions, and always conclude with the statement that the man cannot be allowed to enter yet. The man, who has equipped himself with many things for his journey, parts with all he has, however valuable, in the hope of bribing the door-keeper. The door-keeper accepts it all, saying, however, as he takes each gift: 'I take this only to keep you from feeling that you have left something undone.' During all these long years the man watches the door-keeper almost incessantly. He forgets about the other door-keepers, and this one seems to him the only barrier between himself and the Law. In the first years he curses his evil fate aloud; later, as he grows old, he only mutters to himself. He grows childish, and since in his prolonged watch he has learned to know even the fleas in the door-keeper's fur collar, he begs the very fleas to help him and to persuade the door-keeper to change his mind. Finally, his eyes grow dim and he does not know whether the world is really darkening around him or whether his eyes are only deceiving him. But in the darkness he can now perceive a radiance that streams immortally from the door of the Law. Now his life is drawing to a close. Before he dies, all that he has experienced during the whole time of his sojourn condenses in his mind into one question, which he has never yet put to the door-keeper. He beckons the door-keeper, since he can no longer raise his stiffening body. The door-keeper has to bend far down to hear him, for the difference in size between them has increased very much to the man's disadvantage. 'What do you want to know now?' asks the door-keeper, 'you are insatiable.' 'Everyone strives to attain the Law,' answers the man, 'how does it come about, then, that in all these years no one has come seeking admittance but me?' The door-keeper perceives that the man is at the end of his strength and his hearing is failing, so he bellows in his ear: 'No one but you could gain admittance through this door, since this door was intended only for you. I am now going to shut it.'

Kafka's man from the country was guilty of living an unlived life, of waiting for permission from others to do what he wanted to do, of not seizing his life and going through the doors intended for him alone. As a result he 'died like a dog'.

In sum

In effect, individuals really have no choice in life but to live with the anxiety of crossing Rubicons if they are to use their potential and avoid their own stagnation, and that of their organisation along with it.

Living in a constant state of existential anxiety requires courage. The courage to address the promises individuals make to themselves at 3.00 in the morning, whilst driving along a sunny road, whilst abroad on holiday, sitting 'alone' at a PC surrounded by colleagues. The problem is that by the morning, by the time they've stopped the car, arrived back in the airport or driven home from the office, in the absence of certainty of what the outcome of their decision will be, back come their doubts and fears. They avoid taking action because of the risks incumbent in the ambiguity of change.

To take the apparently safe path of allowing others to make our decisions for us, leads not only to pointlessness but also to a sense powerlessness, hopelessness, helplessness and quiet desperation. It's feelings such as these that typify the overall attitude and demeanour of many people in organisations today, and produces the climate of lethargy, inertia, depression and low morale. The stress created by feeling undervalued, unrecognised and powerless is horrendous. On the other hand, having the courage to do what we believe in and deal with the consequences will also cause anxiety, but will give the satisfaction of knowing that we are living an authentic life.

Our existence requires our constantly making decisions about life as it is experienced, and acting on those decisions. The result of being confronted with decisions is a constant choice between *existential anxiety* (fear of doing something with unknown outcomes) and *existential guilt* (the realisation that by not acting we are passively giving up our birthright by failing to use our potential).

Whilst existential anxiety is both stressful and developmental, existential guilt is stressful and corrosive. The most dynamic approach to life is to continually act and accept the inevitable existential anxiety. To live life fully is to continuously experience existence on the 'cutting edge of time' (Pirsig, 1974).

_____ **Self-Analysis** _____

Crossing Rubicons

Think of something that is troubling you right now. Look at the model of change in Figure 9, and choose at which point(s) you are blocked.

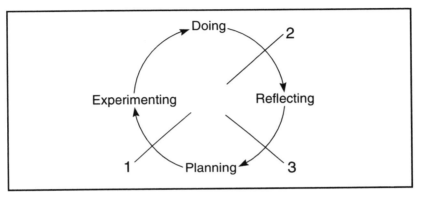

Figure 9   The model of change

- How are you blocking yourself?
- What choices do you have?
- What are you telling yourself to avoid taking the risk of change? Your catastrophic fantasies?
- What is the worst thing that can happen?
- Is it really that bad?
- Is it really likely to happen?
- What is the best thing that can happen?
- What will happen if you don't take the risk?
- Do you want to live with the guilt (and stress) of standing still in life or the anxiety of fulfilling your potential through change and development?

6 If Freedom of Choice is Only 'an Illusion', why Encourage Autonomy?

‘The ultimate purpose of man is not merely to fly from Chicago to London in seven hours, eating a ten course dinner en-route. The great goal of man is not simply to create a sleek and self-satisfied culture of comfort, leisure and fun . . . The final measure of greatness is whether you and I have increased the freedom of man [and] enhanced [his] dignity.’ (*Herbert Pronchow*)

Assumptions about human nature and how people learn

Neither those who continue to sabotage the culture nor those who acquiesce in politics are taking the risk of crossing a Rubicon. There are those who want to get on with their jobs, be excellent, achieve organisational goals and self-actualise and Chapters 7–14 will describe how to help them to cross these Rubicons. Then there are those who don't want to conform to the desired norms; I'll review the reasons for this now.

Very often, when a change programme is proposed it is obvious, right from the start, that some of the management team have very cynical views about the programme and the ideal culture advocated. This cynicism isn't shallow or just a matter of being plain bloody-minded. We are asking people to make fundamental changes to underlying assumptions about human nature and how people learn. They intuitively don't agree with these assumptions, but not necessarily at a conscious level.

When a culture change programme is proposed as a solution to organisational problems, the Managing Director and Board are led to believe that the current culture ('the actual culture') is hindering effectiveness. The ideal solution ('the ideal culture') is one where cooperation, communication and use of creative potential leads to increased revenue and profit as in the case of Harlow systems. The way to achieve the ideal is by changing the culture of the organisation to one where individuals feel free to experiment with new ideas and behaviours (creating a safe and supportive environment). In other words they are sold the ideal–actual model in Figure 10. This is what they buy into. And who wouldn't?

However, underlying this model of change are inescapable assumptions about human nature and how people learn. If individuals are to commit to creating such an environment they have to understand and commit also to these core assumptions.

Yet in some cases we are asking managers to create a liberal environment based on a philosophy of human nature, learning and development that many wouldn't even create for their own children in their own home! For example, some people allow their children to have free access to sweets because they trust them to regulate themselves. Others believe that children cannot be trusted to do the right thing and need to be controlled. The same applies to management style. It depends on your view of human nature. Often, the liberal approach is foisted onto CEOs, MDs, executives and managers who secretly think it's a load of hogwash but are either unclear of what they *do* think, afraid to say what

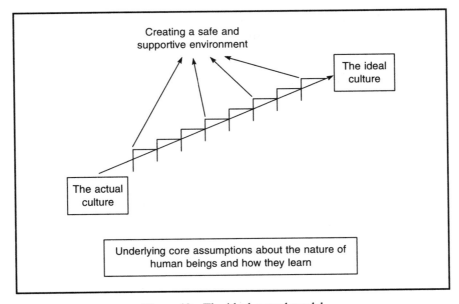

Figure 10 The ideal–actual model

they do think or remain unconvinced but find the external consultants so
intriguing that they're prepared to give anything a try once.

Had the consultants gone into the Board explicitly stating the
underlying model of human behaviour on which their culture change
programme was based and explained how the entire company including
the Board had to change their behaviour:

- One-third would have said: 'No way – it's not what I believe and not
  what I want.'
- One-third would have said: 'That's an interesting viewpoint, I'd like to
  try.'
- One-third would have said: 'I want that. That's me.'

> It is impossible to understand the structure and climate created by
> each individual manager within their department without first
> understanding their beliefs and assumptions – their vision – of the
> nature of human beings and how they learn.

For example, a manager who leads by a 'carrot and stick' approach
carries a different set of assumptions from a manager who uses a
'collaborative, team-working' style of leadership.

Strangely, whereas many believe that given the freedom to chose *they*
are free to act in a responsible manner, they see their subordinates as
irresponsible and determined either by internal (innate) instincts or
external rewards and punishments! Since our internalised model of
human nature will affect the way we attempt to motivate, control and
develop people, it seems to me that if we want to manage people we can't
go around with such contradictory beliefs.

This is especially true since Organisation Development is all about
management taking the lead in creating an environment that makes
certain assumptions about how to develop potential. For example,
Excellence, TQM, BPR and Learning Environments are all a shorthand
way of subscribing to Humanistic assumptions. Indeed, the very idea that
we *have* potential to develop is an assumption that some models of
human nature make and others do not.

So what are these different assumptions about human nature and
learning?

Basic assumptions and management style

Though largely outmoded today, a good starting point is McGregor's model (1960), in which he categories the assumptions we make about human nature into Theory X and Theory Y, as shown in Table 4.

According to McGregor, those managers who use rewards and threats – the 'carrot and stick' approach – are working with what he calls *Theory X assumptions* about human nature. They feel that you must use external controls to deal with all staff who would be unreliable, irresponsible and immature if you let them. This is the *deterministic* view of human nature.

Those managers who believe in self-motivation make *Theory Y assumptions* about human nature. If you create an environment which is encouraging, positive, provides recognition, allows for mistakes and provides challenge and personal development individuals will motivate themselves to achieve company goals. This approach sees human beings as having *free will*.

As I have said before, some managers believe that while they themselves are responsible and free to act accordingly (Theory Y), all others are not (Theory X). This may sound reasonable but it's illogical to argue that you are free to weigh up alternatives, make decisions and choose your course of action whilst others are controlled by external

Table 4   McGregor's Theory X and Theory Y assumptions about human nature

Theory X	Theory Y
1 Work is inherently distasteful to most people	1 Work is as natural as play, if the conditions are favourable, and can be inherently satisfying
2 Most people are not ambitious, have little desire for responsibility and prefer to be directed	2 Self-control is often indispensable in achieving organisational goals
3 Most people have little capacity for creativity in solving organisational problems	3 The capacity for creativity in solving organisational problems is widely distributed in the population
4 Motivation occurs only at the physiological and security levels of Maslow's Need Hierarchy	4 Motivation, occurs at the social, esteem and self-actualisation levels, as well as the physiological and security levels
5 Most people must be closely controlled and often forced to achieve organisational objectives.	5 People can be self-directed and creative at work if properly motivated.

stimuli or internal innate predispositions. Either human beings are free or they are determined. Which is it?

Clarifying this point is crucial because when management say they will support a culture which encourages people to feel free to make choices, act autonomously, be creative and so on, they need to be clear that such an approach is based upon Theory Y assumptions. Those who have not thought through their own beliefs may find that, because they have Theory X assumptions, it is difficult to give people the freedom that this change requires. As a result they may unwittingly sabotage the process by continuing to over control others due to lack of trust and fear of their own lack of control:

As a client said to me: 'What is the point of creating an environment where people have freedom to do what they think best when I believe that people are generally untrustworthy and need to be controlled?'

So, the question is: are we free to weigh up alternatives, make decisions and choose our own course of action, or not? Is human nature best described by Theory X or by Theory Y?

The assumption of determinism

For hundreds of years philosophers, theologians and scientists have questioned whether we are active, responsible agents with 'free will' or puppets determined by forces beyond our control whose behaviour follows laws of cause and effect. Whereas our intellectual thought process may believe a deterministic view of the universe and other humans' behaviour, our gut feel leads us to the belief that we personally have free will, since we see ourselves as able to choose. For example in cases of mass murder, like that of the Dunblane massacre, the common presentation is that the individual was innately evil, that you cannot blame parents or upbringing, that in other words he was predetermined to act as he did. Yet, if any one of those who believed this were asked 'Would you have done the same thing?', they would surely reply: 'Of course not, I know the difference between right and wrong.' In other words, they would argue that whilst they have freedom of choice in all their actions he does not.

Two models of human behaviour commonly used in management training, implicitly but rarely explicitly, are the psychoanalytic and behaviouristic. Both imply that behaviour is determined.

According to the orthodox psychoanalytic model based on the work of Sigmund Freud, behaviour is determined by irrational forces, unconscious motivations, biological and instinctual drives as these evolve through key psycho-sexual stages of development. As Freud (1953) said:

> 'Man is lived by the unconscious . . . The deeply rooted belief in psychic freedom and choice is quite unscientific and must give ground before the claims of a determinism which governs mental life.'

Whereas psychoanalysts believe that we are *innately* irrational, lazy and selfish, *behaviourists* believe the opposite is true. Those who transgress society's moral code do so because of their history of *external* rewards and punishments: freedom of choice is only 'an illusion'.

According to strict behaviourism, the brain is a '*tabula rasa*' (an empty slate) onto which all knowledge is written, an 'empty vessel' having no prior nature. Behaviourists see the individual as a passive element and learning as automatic, gradual and 'forced upon' the organism by the external demands of reward and punishment. Since the environment is solely responsible for all behaviour, it follows that through appropriate environmental control one could condition a healthy personality. Behaviour which is good or evil, rational or irrational, depends upon the individual's conditioning. The maintenance and modification of behaviour become exclusively a matter of changing the patterns of *rewards* and *punishments*. B. F. Skinner (1953), has emphasised that he is not trying to take away our freedom since we are not free anyway:

> 'The hypotheses that man is not free is essential to the application of the scientific method to the study of human behaviour.'

Skinner (1971) advocates that we should abandon our illusory beliefs in behavioural freedom, accept the inevitability of control and design an environment in which behaviour will be directed towards socially desirable ends, exclusively through the use of positive reinforcement. This is the key to the imaginary utopia described in his novel *Walden Two* (1948). Like many managers, Skinner finds no contradiction in the idea that a few more powerful individuals have the apparent free will to design such a totalitarian environment and decide what is right and wrong!

Whether they are aware of it or not, many individuals have Theory X, behaviourist or psychoanalytic assumptions about human nature, learning and the ideal environment. They believe that:

- *rules* should be rigid, conform to convention and changes in them must conform to established patterns.
- *others* are not to be trusted
- *interactions* are controlling, critical and dishonest
- *intergroup relations* are competitive, suspicious and prejudiced.

These assumptions are expressed in their opinions on how to deal with criminals, disruptive school children, babies who won't sleep, dogs that need house training and the women or men they live with.

Managers with these assumptions are not interested in creating a climate in which individuals can maximise personal choices, discover their own truths and 'become'. Instead, they devote their time to giving instructions, establishing goals, setting objectives, implementing strategies, measuring activities, modelling appropriate behaviours and providing reinforcement for 'good' behaviour, the achievement of objectives and goal attainment. They may be supportive but are likely to regard the establishment of any form of relationship as simply a means of gaining behavioural control. The relationship is by no means considered to be central to change in the way it is in the humanistic approach of culture change programmes.

The assumption of freedom

In our own personal lives probably none of us believes in a strict determinism. Our whole way of life with its freedom of discussion, ballot boxes, democratic traditions and personal responsibility in law, is based heavily on the assumption that we are capable of *self-determination*. Our common sense view is that we choose what we do and determine our own course of action and must, therefore, have free will.

Free will is inextricably linked to the concept of *responsibility*. We hold people to be morally or legally responsible for what they do and believe that they 'cause' their own behaviour and are not driven by internal or external drives. Criminal law rests on the assumption that people have free will and that, if they do wrong, they have *chosen* to do so, are blameworthy, and should therefore be punished.

In fact an authoritarian society is considered by us to be a pathological one. The fact that efforts both by communist and fascist societies and organisations have never been wholly or lastingly successful seems to indicate a basic human need to be spiritual, evaluative and active rather than simply robotic, passive and reactive.

The humanistic–existential perspective is both an outgrowth of and a reaction to the psychoanalytic perspective. Indeed many early thinkers such as Frankl and Perls were trained as psychoanalysts and have retained certain basic assumptions. Yet, both psychoanalysis and behaviourism came to seem inadequate because of the deterministic idea that human action is the product of forces beyond the control (indeed often beyond the knowledge) of the individual. Humanists believe that:

- *rules* are flexible and can change as and when the need arises
- *others* have the best of intentions
- *interactions* are nurturing, caring and honest
- *intergroup relations* are supportive, cooperative and unprejudiced.

Rarely are we conscious of how our values influence our attitudes and we probably could not voice them even if asked. These values are played out in other ways.

For example, I was at a meeting where the Company's Sales Director, Tim Jeffreys, was attempting to get Peter James, the Professional Services Director, to realise that if the customer wants something now all the stops need to be pulled out to get it done. Tim is a salesman at heart and gets his positive self-concept from being cavalier, breaking all the rules, making things happen. He values these things and those who do them. Peter, on the other hand, being a 'techy' at heart values caution, following rules and taking as long as it takes to do the job right.

Beneath the surface of their battle to get the job done is their 'shoulds', 'oughts' and 'musts' about what is the right way and the wrong way to do things and to behave with others. Their personal values are very much the process issue in this debate but without process facilitation the chances are they would never get raised. So the discussion about the task comes to an uneasy end with each believing the other is an incompetent fool and that they themselves are right. And nothing changes.

Rogers and Skinner (1956) conducted a celebrated symposium on the question of the *control of human behaviour* in which the two clearly delineated the differences between the humanistic and the behaviouristic approaches to psychology: the differences were fundamental and irreconcilable. The basic difference between the two lies in their views of what humans are and what they ought to be, as shown in Table 5.

Table 5   Three views of human nature

Approach	Good/Evil	Rational/Irrational	Free/Determined
Psychoanalytic	Evil	Irrational	Determined
Behaviouristic	Neutral	Depends on learning	Determined
Humanistic–Existential	*Good*	*Rational*	*Free choice*

In sum

We all work from a psychological theory of human nature, though we may not be able to express it explicitly. We may believe people are naturally lazy and evil, or hard working and good. We may believe that to develop as social beings they need harsh control or understanding, tolerance and love. We may not voice this as a coherent theory but such attitudes and values are displayed in our approach to others in terms of how flexible or rigid, how controlling or collaborative, how friendly or distant, how supportive or critical, how accepting or judgmental we are.

The one-third of the company who do not and will never fit the culture would have been authentic had they said: 'No way, it's not what I believe and it's not what I want', and refused to change. It's unrealistic and unfair to expect people who have held these views for 30 or 40 years to change in a couple of 2-day workshops.

The management is therefore faced with two choices:

(a)   They can ring fence these managers to ensure that their attitudes and behaviours do not poison the new culture by ensuring that they behave in such a way as to support the new culture even if they do not believe in it.
(b)   They can be asked to leave.

It is highly likely that those having to live with the first option will leave anyway.

A second group would fit into the middle third, who combine both humanistic and behaviouristic approaches and are interested in the approach of culture change programmes and are willing to try. They think they are sure where they stand and voice their opinion strongly yet contradict themselves with their behaviour. I know an MD who is extremely autocratic, secretive and controlling at home with his wife and sons, yet is warm, caring, supportive and open with his staff.

The final one-third are genuinely humanistic at heart yet conform to the negative norms of the culture and acquiesce with the saboteurs and the company politics. I know an extremely right-wing conservative MP who believes in corporal punishment, bringing back the birch and in the concept of short sharp shocks for those who transgress the law, yet he has brought up his own daughter, now a highly successful law abiding professional herself, in a warm, positive, humanistic environment. He would not dream of attempting to develop her personality or potential in a Skinnerian environment.

Before anyone embarks on a culture change programme it seems essential that they first understand the assumptions about human nature and learning that underlie the consultant's model and dictate their view of the ideal leadership style and climate. Next, they need to understand their own assumptions, and finally they need to make clear to everyone in the organisation that it is these assumptions that they are committing themselves to if they are to join in the creation of the appropriate environment to change behaviour. If managers or employees do not hold humanistic assumptions, the money and effort will be wasted. But, worse, the failure of the programme will provide the evidence for those with psychoanalytic/behaviouristic/Theory X assumptions to deepen their cynical attitudes and revert back to type.

The one-third who don't hold humanistic values will try to pull the culture back to the one they believe most effectively allows them to manage and motivate staff and colleagues. The others prefer to reach a consensus with them in spite of the fact that after a change programme they will have developed the group dynamic knowledge, self-awareness and skills that should enable them to confront the saboteurs.

Chapter 7 describes situations where, had they chosen to cross the Rubicon by using these skills to confront the company politics played by those who refuse to change, they could have changed the culture.

7 Confronting the Cycle of Group Dynamics and Company Politics

'Why, you may take the most gallant sailor, the most intrepid airman or the most audacious soldier, put them at a table together – what do you get? The sum of their fears.'

(*Winston Churchill*)

'Everything was going fine, and then someone had a *feeling*'

Many of the contacts with others in organisations are dishonest, unfriendly and even downright hostile. When individuals assert their opinion, listen to the opinions of others and find mutually acceptable solutions there is no problem with communication. Problems arise when individuals use words not to achieve their task but for other purposes such as to:

- manipulate
- confuse
- obstruct
- dominate
- punish
- mock
- belittle
- patronise

- soothe
- put down
- score a point
- divide and rule
- gain popularity
- deceive
- defer
- reject.

When people use words for political game-playing, conversations become stilted, distorted and ineffective. Individuals feel uncomfortable, resentful or resigned. They begin to lose touch with solving the organisational issue in an attempt to maintain their integrity and defend their ego in a subversively hostile environment.

Even so, many refuse to appreciate that the way people *feel* will affect the way they behave. If the flow of conversation is interrupted to raise these process issues that block task achievement the attitude is one of 'everything was going fine and then someone had a *feeling*'! Well

70

someone had a *feeling* when everything was going fine. That's why it was going fine. They were having a *feeling* of being included, of being listened to, of being liked, of being taken seriously, of competence.

You cannot get away from feelings. When an individual says 'everything was going fine and then someone had a *feeling*', that statement in itself and the strength and tone of voice with which it is made is coming out of a *feeling*. The feeling is probably one of exasperation at someone interfering with their game which is designed to win personal power and control. Have you ever noticed how the quiet members of the group are always relieved to see someone stop the meeting at that point?

For someone to assume that feelings are not involved when everything is going fine or that individuals can divorce their feelings from anything they do is not only a ridiculously naive approach to human behaviour but also a complete denial of the source of their own motivations and mood swings.

The three circles model of group dynamics

How can individuals recognise, surface and deal with the political game-playing in groups? Adair in his book *Effective Leadership* (1983) made famous the *three circles model of group dynamics* in terms of leadership:

> *Teachers on group dynamics courses used a three circles model to illustrate the three areas of need. It appeared in duplicated notes which formed the corpus of 'theory' in those pioneer days, but as far as I know it was never printed. So nobody knows who first imagined this brilliant and simple model.* (p. 33)

The *three areas of need* in every group, be it in the organisation as a whole, the department, the team or one-to-one interactions, are:

> (1) *Task needs* e.g. defining the task, checking resources, setting standards and managing time
> (2) *Group maintenance needs* e.g. encouraging, sharing responsibility, coordinating, reconciling conflict and answering questions
> (3) *Individual needs* e.g. listening, recognising efforts, respecting, stretching, coaching and consulting.

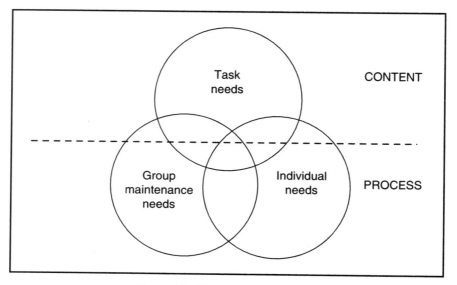

Figure 11   The three circles model

The three circles model of group dynamics is shown in Figure 11.

Satisfaction of one need affect performance of the other two

The three circles overlap because each has an effect on the other. *Individual* needs are more or less those of Maslow's need hierarchy (see Chapter 4). When individuals don't feel liked, competent, listened to, rewarded, supported, recognised, or that they are developing themselves both personally and professionally, they no longer want to belong to the *group*, be it the team, department or organisation, nor do they feel motivated to achieve the *task*.

If, on the other hand, they are made to feel isolated from the *group*, because certain individuals are ganging up against them, or they have different values and attitudes, or most of their time is spent off-site, their *individual* needs for recognition, a sense of belonging, being listened to and encourage and so on are not satisfied and so once again they do not feel motivated to creatively achieve the *task*.

Finally, if individuals are working with a manager, team, department or organisation that is not focused on achieving the *task* needs, they cannot achieve their *individual* needs of competence, personal and professional development, self-actualisation, achievement, recognition and so on and so no longer want to be a part of that *group*.

There are, of course, times when people cannot be focused on all three needs to the same extent, for example when the organisation has a huge order to deliver in a limited amount of time. If the team has paid attention to group and individual needs during quieter times, they are likely to pull out all the stops during a crisis after which they can be sure that their efforts, both as a team and individually, will be recognised. If, however, individual and group needs are rarely attended to, what will happen when the company asks them to attend to the task needs in crisis mode? Very little, probably.

Raising group dynamic issues

When a group is ineffective, as was previously mentioned, management first look to change organisational issues such as the rules, procedures or systems in order to solve the process issues. In teamworking, members attending a meeting will often blame their lack of progress on the fact that they have not set an agenda, not defined their objectives, do not have a leader, have not been well briefed prior to the meeting and so on. These are the task needs and are *content issues*.

Yet more often than not, to an outside observer, it is clear that the real issue is that either group needs or individual needs are not being met. The reason that they are not making progress with the task is that people feel bad. They may feel bad about each other, the leadership style, the decision-making processes, the tone of the conversation and so on. These are the process issues and it is the process issues that make up the *dynamics of the group*.

Process issues are the result of expectations not being met. Individuals have certain views about how the task should be achieved and how individual and group needs should be met which they expect the group to satisfy. For example, someone who thinks meetings 'should' have a leader, a clear time frame and an agenda will continually sabotage until that issue is discussed. Or when a member values acting on an agreed decision and finds others still evaluating the risks, he will attempt to short circuit or close down the discussion in order to meet his need for action.

If the group does not recognise and respect the individual's expectations, then one of the following will manifest itself as the focal group process issue (Blake and Mouton, 1983):

1	*Power and control*:	Fighting for leadership and control over the content and direction of the meeting
2	*Morale and cohesion*:	Opting out, psychologically or physically leaving, lack of involvement and disappointment at both the way the meeting is being run and with other members of the group
3	*Norms and standards*:	Disagreeing with the way the meeting is being run or the proposed way of actioning a decision
4	*Goals and objectives*:	Blocking progress in the meeting or consensus decisions because of differences in personal or departmental agendas.

These focal issues are unstated and not obvious from the content of the conversation, but block progress on the task. Whenever there is dissension in the group or even when the content of the discussion appears to be perfectly innocuous but everyone is conscious that the conversation is going nowhere, then one of these four focal issues it is likely to be involved.

'Team spirited' versus 'mean spirited'

Everyone suffers to some extent if their individual and group needs are not satisfied but some people suffer more than others and some people never seem to be able to put their ego to one side and focus on the task. Rather than raise the focal issue, individuals hide their real feelings and resort to the following behaviours that typify teamworking:

- Personal agendas
- Opting out
- Point scoring
- Ego defensive behaviour
- Not listening
- Aggressive behaviour
- Lying
- Fear
- Blaming
- Cynicism
- Passivity
- Avoidance
- Manipulation
- Shallow agreements
- Broken commitments
- Non-cooperation.

When this kind of ego-defensive game-playing occurs in the top team, the rest of the organisation feels empowered to perpetuate the same attitudes, values and behaviour throughout the organisation and a *culture of intra-* and *interdepartmental non-cooperation* develops.

It follows, therefore, that such behaviour will apply to daily interactions at all levels throughout the organisation. Eventually those with their 'eye on the ball' and displaying the positive norms of pleasing management and achieving company goals become demoralised by a lack of clearly stated top-down support and overpowered by those peers who sabotage their efforts by acting out the negative norms.

Each of these behaviours is reviewed below with the typical group solution which is to acquiesce and the preferred solution to be adopted if individuals are to confront the company politics. Each preferred solution involves Level 1 and 2 skills, but the courage required to raise the issue involves the Level 3 (see Chapter 2) approach to personal responsibility, freedom and choice.

(a)   Personal agendas

Most meetings have at least one member who is working from a personal rather than a group agenda – perfectionists, for example, who are preoccupied with details, rules, schedules and the like. This personal agenda makes them unable to discard obsolete ideas, procedures or rules even if they have no current value and can block projects getting finished or decisions being made. Others manipulate the situation to their own ends no matter what others think:

Julie Williams

During a strategy meeting, Julie Williams, the accountant, was asked to take notes. Towards the end of the meeting she was asked to present the agreed action plans. The team was astonished to discover that she had written actions that had been discussed and rejected but that reflected Julie's ideas and suggestions.

Group solution: The team members acquiesced to her action plan during the meeting and restated their own plans to each other in corridor meetings which produced confusion as to what exactly had been agreed. Ultimately this behaviour resulted in a lack of trust and cooperation between them.

Preferred solution: As she presented the actions someone could ask: 'What happened there, Julie?' Julie will say, with wide-eyed innocence 'What?' They reply 'You've written actions that we didn't agree. What's that about, Julie?' Whatever her response, the issue to discuss is her personal agenda. They then move to personal agendas as a group issue. The team needed to get agreement that if people's ideas are not accepted they must agree to disagree to consensus decisions. They must also drop their personal agendas and work with the group action plans if the team was to be effective.

Many people have been through workshops and learnt these group dynamic and interpersonal skills but cannot find the courage to put them into practice. Learning to live with the anxiety of action is rarely considered in such workshops. Yet without dealing with this issue, all the knowledge in the world won't change anything.

(b)   Opting out

Some individuals feel so anxious, threatened or angry that they opt out. They may be quiet for long periods of time or pull their chair away from the circle and so remove themselves not only from discussion but from owning any decisions made in the discussion. They may use jokes, go to the toilet, leave to make a phone call, or suggest a cigarette break. All these things may be a cry for help rather than the real wish to leave the room or the discussion. While they doodle, go to 'sleep' or look out of the window they may have a thoughtful or cynical look on their face. Recognising the signs, and helping the person become involved once, more is an important group dynamic skill:

Jim Duncan

At a sales review meeting Jim Duncan, a sales executive, had a bee in his bonnet. He wanted to pay an incentive to the sales force of their supplier. The sales manager, Roger Pearl, said this had absolutely been vetoed by the supplier's senior management who treated it in the same light as unsolicited payments. As such it was non-negotiable and out of his control. From then on, unless directly involved, Jim opted out of the meeting by either doodling or using phone messages as an excuse to leave the meeting for long periods of time effectively stopping the meeting until his return.

Group solution: Roger either said nothing about the telephone calls taking coffee breaks, and talking about other things and ignored the doodling or stopped the conversation until Jim was forced to stop doodling and respond to the silence directed at him. The result was wasted time, bad feelings about both Jim and Roger and irritation. By the end, Jim felt stupid and still hadn't let go of the problem at 6.30 that night in corridor meetings.

Preferred solution: Roger could have confronted the behaviour by asking Jim what the doodling was about. To which Jim would have replied: 'nothing.' Roger could then have said: 'It feels as if you've left the meeting', at which time Jim might feel OK about raising his issues again. Roger could have pointed to the lengthy phone calls and made the same point. Hoping to ignore Jim's tantrums simply disrupts the meeting, loses respect and has the potential for a revenge cycle as described in 'point scoring' below.

(c)   Point scoring

Very rarely do individuals get away with trampling on people's feelings. They usually get back at each other one way or the other. This kind of point scoring is called a 'revenge cycle', and it may take minutes, hours, days or years but some people are heavily involved in satisfying their revenge.

Revenge cycles often occur when someone's idea is rejected in such a way that he feels foolish. If you watch him he will wait until the other person makes a point and no matter how reasonable and useful it is, the aggrieved team member will vehemently and insensitively disagree:

Harry Trimble

Harry Trimble is the CEO of a charity. Of the 6 on the Board of Management, 4 voted for him and 2 voted for another candidate. Every time something goes slightly wrong, these 2 Board members say that it wouldn't have happened if the Board had chosen the candidate they favoured. They are in a revenge cycle. This explains why he is having so much difficulty with the confirmation of his contract.

This revenge cycle of scoring points is common and it is the *causal issue* of two Board members feeling disgruntled that needs to be raised and dealt with not the *symptom* – such as the contract in Harry's case.

(d)   Ego-defensive behaviour

It's very easy to 'scapegoat' another member of the group, ascribing blame for some event. In other cases, the group will scapegoat someone who has dared to express some anxiety, admit difficulty or confusion. If the leader is not careful, everyone will become hooked on this golden opportunity to hide their own feelings and problems. It's a harrowing experience, as anyone who has been on the receiving end will know.

Another way groups can 'scapegoat' is that, rather than looking at their own shortcomings, they find it much less threatening to blame someone, or some 'body' outside themselves – such as the economic climate, the supplier, senior management, the City, the subordinates or the customers! This 'running away' needs to be acknowledged and the focus of attention brought back into the group.

(e)   Not listening

Someone's individual or team needs may not be satisfied because:

- their point was over-talked
- their point was thrown out
- they feel unable to make a point
- others are playing the usual power games
- the leader is threatening
- the leader has favourites, and they are not one of them.

As a result of not being listened to they stop listening or speaking yet there is no lack of communication! Feelings ooze out of silent members of the team as they read newspapers, stand up to get coffee or avoid eye contact. Others express that they feel peeved by interrupting or chatting to the person next to them. Whatever the signs, if corridor meetings are to be avoided, it is imperative that what is *not* being said is picked up on:

Mark Adams

Mark Adams, a production manager in the UK, was very popular with his team. Jean-Paul Le-Maitre was from France and had just been promoted above Mark's head into the new post of Northern European Production Director. At their first team meeting Mark spent most of the time chatting across the table, reading a newspaper, standing up to get coffee and trying to incorporate the external facilitators in the game by grinning and mocking Jean-Paul. He had gone 'psychologically', not only from the content of the meeting, but from the organisation.

Group solution: Jean-Paul attempted to win support and interest by remaining friendly. Mark found this even more amusing since, coming out of a competitive frame of mind, those who resolve conflict through collaboration are seen as 'wet'. The more Jean-Paul tried to be nice the more Mark thought he'd won and so he continued his behaviour all the more.

Preferred solution: If Mark has his head down reading the newspaper Jean-Paul could say: 'Mark, I'm wondering what your thinking right now.' Mark would look up with an insolent expression and pretend surprise but smile and say, 'What?', as if he doesn't know what Jean-Paul's talking about. Jean-Paul could repeat: 'I'm wondering what you're thinking right now?' And Mark would say, 'What?' Jean-Paul would wait. If he got no response, he would own the problem and say: 'I find it difficult to work in this group when you're reading the paper or chatting and so on. It feels to me as if you are not interested in what we're saying.' Mark could not deny Jean-Paul's feelings and would be unable to ignore them since his game is that he's the nice guy. It would therefore be pretty difficult to play the 'I've gone psychologically' game again without looking like the bad one.

In these situations it's important to *label the game*. This helps to stick to discussing the process issues rather than the content issue, otherwise Mark's sabotage technique would have worked since he is now back in the chair expounding a view that he didn't expound 20 minutes ago, either because he was over-talked, out-argued or chose not to raise it. Whatever the case, the point of *this* discussion is that when he does not get his own way his sabotage technique is to 'mock' those in power. That's his game. Bringing others into the picture who have done the same will mean that Mark can feel able to change without losing face.

If Jean-Paul has a hunch that the *real* part of not getting his own way was the fact that Mark did not get his job then this leadership issue needs to be dealt with otherwise it will continue to be played out through each item on the agenda, and with it Jean-Paul.

(f)   Aggression, passivity and fear

Some individuals who feel anxious, threatened or angry may deal with these feelings by dominating others and being *aggressive*. This makes them feel less threatened and therefore safer. The *passive* members may say little for *fear* of being publicly abused, but have no intention of following decisions made by an autocrat who has no formal power and authority. Even if meetings look as if they working well a state of total anarchy can occur outside the meeting room once each department manager or team member returns to their own section:

Hugh Sykes

Hugh Sykes, the Financial Controller, came from a large multinational corporate environment and valued well defined procedures and a disciplined work force. David Wotton, the sales manager, was new to the job and valued a 'can-do', 'problem-solving', 'quick fix' mentality. There were constant battles in different guises over the difference in values, but each example was dealt with in content rather than process terms. For example, Hugh wanted to institute strict credit control and debt collection procedures specifically on one major client at the same time that David was trying to negotiate a renewal of the contract under very difficult circumstances. Whenever Hugh, who was quiet and diffident, tried to argue his point, David would lose his temper and shout. Those of the management team who came out of a sales service background sided with David and those who did not sided with Hugh.

Group solution: Because the MD sympathised with both viewpoints he saw no way to square the circle. Instead he tried both to calm the anger and modify the views in corridor meetings. This did not work. In the next meeting the process repeated itself over a different issues when once again Hugh was out-shouted and out-talked by David.

Preferred solution: The group does not have to wait for the MD to act while everyone else looks on. The MD or any other member of the team could have said: 'It seems to me that the way you both argue a point always ends up with David shouting and Hugh sulking. As a result nothing is ever agreed between you. What's it all about?' They will immediately start to get into the content of the discussion. At which point he can say: 'No I don't want to get back into the same pattern of behaviour. I want to discuss the pattern of behaviour. Every time you discus something, David shouts down Hugh who sulks and nothing gets resolved, the meeting becomes split into factions and it is dealt with outside the meeting. This is not working. How do the rest of you feel.' This takes the pressure off them and someone less emotionally involved can say how it affects them.

An effective process intervention is one that asks an *innocuous question* in the right *tone of voice*. You can say the words: 'What's it all about?' as if you have no preconceived ideas, are not judging anyone and genuinely want to understand the problem. Or you can say, 'What's it all about?' as if you assume you know exactly what the problem is, you have no intention of understanding another point of view and that they had better cut it out or else. The latter approach will not encourage honest discussion and resolution of interpersonal or group conflicts!

In such disputes as these David could be encouraged to take the risk of speaking less and listening more. It is just as uncomfortable for verbose team members to keep quiet as it is for quiet members to speak out. And

Hugh could be encouraged to take the risk of being more forceful about those issues he feels strongly about. Using language such as win–lose helps. Rather than shut up or shout back when David is expounding his views, in the future, after this discussion, group members can simply say: 'I feel as if we're back into win–lose between you two.' This should shorten the time on each new occasion between picking up on the game and re-establishing the 'win–win' behaviours in the group.

(g) Lying

There may be some who use lies to back up their position. No matter how you ask, when you ask or what you ask, they always have a reason why it can't be done. Lies can sabotage work. People may lie with rules, procedures, overload of work or statistics, but you know it's a lie:

Jeremy Turner

In a public utilities company, whilst trying to win a point against Joan Webster, a personnel officer, an engineer, Jeremy Turner, stated that *everyone* knows that 13.45 per cent of all the data entered into any system is incorrect due to operator error. Because of this he argued that the statistics being used by the HR department about his staff were unreliable. Joan knew that this was a lie and responded with another lie by saying that her department rechecked every 10 documents and had found no errors. Jeremy then lied again with more data and technical jargon.

Group solution: This conversation went on for some time until a second engineer cut in to defend Joan and the subject was changed. Joan carried on producing the same data and Jeremy carried on ignoring it.

Preferred solution: Joan could have said: 'That's a very interesting statistic and I would like to gather more data myself before we continue this discussion. Can we leave it until the next meeting?' At the next meeting Joan brings in a written set of statistics and tells the group that the statistics quoted by Jeremy were wrong and that she feels that this is a technique frequently used in the group by members trying to make their point – the point in this case being that Jeremy does not like his staff being judged by Joan and the personnel department. This is what now needs to be discussed, not the statistics or the lies. In terms of the focal issue, it began as *goals and objectives* where Jeremy wants to measure his own staff and HR believe it's their job, and became one of *power and control*.

If Joan was aware that the anxiety created by being authentic was no worse than the stress involved in being sabotaged by dishonesty and resorting to dishonesty herself, she would have found it easier to be honest and confront Jeremy's game.

(h) Blaming

Blaming occurs when staff find that something has gone wrong and, rather than find out how to put it right, they focus on attributing blame:

The IT department

A large multiple retail chain was seeking to implement a new IT system that would enable it to know instantly what was being sold at what price, compare prices with other chain stores and make instantaneous changes so as to remain competitive. The project was running 2 years late. The main Board were putting pressure to understand what was happening and the directors and project team of both the IT department and Retail Operations had a meeting to discuss their response. During the meeting each team blamed the other for the failure, using written evidence. The IT department claimed Operations had consistently changed their requirements, while Operations claimed they had to changed their requirements because the IT department consistently failed to deliver what they promised.

Group solution: The meeting was extremely acrimonious, with the noisy members getting heated and personal, whilst the quiet members opted out. As a result, rather than either side influencing the other, each side's views entrenched. Had this been allowed to continue, the chances are that both departments would have been seen as incompetent by the Board, the project would have been contracted out and the IT department outsourced.

Preferred solution: At the height of the heated discussion the 4 focal issues could be written up and group members asked which issue was relevant right now: Power and control, morale and cohesion, norms and standards, goals and objectives. Once the issue is voiced, feelings subside. Someone might say Goals and objectives, whilst others might point to Morale and cohesion or Power and control. The fact is that they are now focusing on the fact that process issues are blocking the task and can begin to deal with these more rationally – beginning, for example, with clarifying common objectives and goals until there is an explicit group consensus.

(i)   Cynicism

The cynical adolescent continues to lurk in some people, who veer between being openly rebellious and sullen and silent.

George Manning

The Vice President of Europe for an IT company, George Manning, was visiting the office in Amsterdam for the first time to introduce his new strategy and vision. Prior to his visit there was tremendous suspicion as to his motives for change especially as he had a reputation of being autocratic and ineffectual. As he was speaking, a young consultant took out a sandwich, unwrapped it and proceeded to eat it. This went unmentioned by George yet his behaviour changed.

Group solution: Rather than raise the issue of the sandwich and apparent disrespect, George's feelings were played out in questions about resources, the new organisation structure, plans for redundancies and so on. He became distant, cold and unyielding on the few points made around the table by anyone who was brave enough to voice an opinion.

Preferred solution: George could have stopped and asked what made the consultant pick up, unwrap and eat the sandwich just then. If the answer was that he was hungry, he could have asked: 'Had I been saying something worthwhile in your eyes I doubt if you'd have satisfied your hunger just at that moment. Do you have a problem with what I am saying?' And sit down. This is a gesture to say: 'I am listening, and I want to know what's on your mind.' You can bet that whatever this guy is cynical about, he is merely acting out the cynicism felt by the rest of the group. If George doesn't get the issues out on the table, he may as well pack up and go home. The basis of the cynicism is the only thing on their mind both before the presentation and after it and so, if George was hoping to motivate the staff, it would have been preferable to pack in the presentation and resolve *this* issue.

The group dynamic skills may seem obvious but as Tom Peters (1982) says:

> ‘Obviously the obvious isn't obvious otherwise everyone would be doing it.’

Knowledge and action are not one and the same, and people need *internal models* which encourage intrepid action in a hostile environment.

(j)   Avoidance

Some individuals will avoid speaking their mind throughout an entire meeting only to hold court just as everyone is about to leave. A leader can fall into the trap of beginning the meeting all over again, which leads to the annoyance of those who hoped to finish on time.

Lily Webb

At the close of a 2½ day management development workshop, after the entire team had been consistently encouraged to raise issues as and when they arose Lily Webb, the Financial Controller, said that she felt very disgruntled about the whole event.

Group solution: Everyone felt bad, said nothing and went home carrying a legacy of anger.

Preferred solution: The issue could have been confronted by saying: 'I really resent the fact that you have waited until we all feel good and are about to go home to tell us that you have been disappointed with our behaviour for 2½ days.' Lily would have started to explain how she felt. She should be stopped and told: 'I am not interested in how you felt on Tuesday. I do not want to re-run the meeting. I am interested in the fact that you chose to raise the issues after the workshop was closed. In fact, this is the way I experience your behaviour in the office sometimes. You make me think you are cooperating with me and then I find you're not.' At this point either someone else will agree – most group behaviour is typical of behaviour in the office – or everyone could be asked how they felt about what had just happened. The conversation needs to revolve around how the team works as a group rather than focusing on Lily, otherwise she will become defensive and get into a revenge cycle.

(k)   Manipulation

When some individuals feel anxious, threatened or angry, rather than say what they mean, they will manipulate the situation to get their own way by *passive aggressive* means. They act as if they are being helpful and charming but there is always a sting in the tail. Even though we have a hunch that individuals are deliberately obstructing us they always have a logical explanation or good excuse for their behaviour.

Passive aggressive behaviour is a much more insidious way of vying for power and control than direct aggression, since it can be denied as deliberate. Indeed if you push your belief that it is, then the blame is turned back on you. This reduces you to a 'lose–win' relationship, because if you ignore their passive aggression you lose and they win and if you confront it, you lose and they win. The only way to resolve the problem is to *confront the game being played*:

Stephen Casey

Carol Charmers had a member of staff, Stephen Casey, who was happy to do the interesting parts of his job but would not complete his boring tasks.

Group solution: On numerous occasions, Carol confronted Stephen about the unfinished tasks. He would smile charmingly, apologise and promise to finish his work, yet he never did.

Preferred solution: Carol needed to label the game Stephen was playing – 'manipulation' – rather than talk about the uncompleted work. Stephen had spent his life manipulating people by being charming and since this habitual form of behaviour had always worked, he was probably no longer conscious that he was doing it. She could tell him that she felt manipulated and didn't like it and ask him what it was about for him. Then ask what they could do about it. Whatever he answers is irrelevant because the purpose of the conversation is to bring the game into the open. As a result it would be very difficult for Stephen to play the same game the following day if Carol, once again, asks him when he was going to finish his tasks.
  If Stephen did attempt to do it again in the future, all Carol needed to say was: 'You're not using the old charm again are you?'

Many complain that to take a member of staff to one side and confront his sabotage technique is a scary prospect, yet it will help them act once they realise that it is equally debilitating to choose to allow this individual's values to control their progress.

(1)   Shallow agreements and broken commitments

In groups it is important to evaluate continually the degree to which people feel free to contribute to the decision-making processes. Otherwise they end up with shallow agreements and hence broken commitments:

- Is anyone feeling pushed out?
- Is someone's opinion lightly dismissed, without good reason?
- Is there a good level of cooperation in the group?
- Is silence taken for agreement?

In many meetings a decision is made *by default*:

'Going to Abilene'

Group solution: 1 person will make a suggestion, 2 people agree, 1 will nod and the other 4 say nothing. 'Agreed', says the first person who writes down the 'decision' and moves onto the next item on the agenda. Is silence usually agreement? Rarely if ever. Silence is usually exactly the opposite yet individuals may be too scared to say so.

Preferred solution: In the above example, 4 people are going to what we call 'Abilene'. There's this lovely story about a couple sitting on the porch of their home near Abilene, Texas with the wife's parents after having had an enormous and successful Sunday lunch. Suddenly the wife, who is tired, hot and enjoying the break feels guilty that her parents are doing nothing and suggests that they drive 15 miles to Abilene for a cream tea. The husband thinks to himself: 'I'm hot and tired but she seems to want to do it so I'd better agree so as not to upset her', and says: 'Great.' The mother, on hearing this, feels the last thing she wants to do is sit in a hot car on a hot and dusty road to sit in some empty cafe and eat again, but she doesn't want to be a party pooper and says: 'What a great idea.' The father is about to drop off to sleep and cannot believe that he is being asked to give up his Sunday afternoon nap but doesn't want to upset his wife and so gets up enthusiastically to go. Having driven for half an hour in the dust and heat all 4 feel annoyed at this imposition on their peaceful afternoon and so none of them join into the spirit of the tea, more or less sitting in silence. Back on the porch hot, full and dirty the wife says: 'Gosh it's great to be back. The last thing I wanted was to go to Abilene.' 'What', says her husband, 'I only went for you.' 'Well I only went because you two seemed so keen.' said the mother. The father didn't need to say anything, he just looked exasperated and fell asleep!

Because 4 people went along with a decision that they were not committed to they merely went though the motions, but had no intentions of doing it right. Had any one of them had the courage to say how they really felt, in all probability the consensus decision which would have satisfied everyone would have been to stay put. People 'go to Abilene' all the time in organisations, making shallow agreements that lead to people going through the motions with broken commitments.

(m)   Non-cooperation

Non-cooperation is apparent in may interactions in groups. The following is an example where instead of just one leader, two people co-lead the group:

Tom Munn

Tom Munn, who was the Vice President of the international division of an American IT company, was invited to join the European Management team which was headed up by Alden Gibson, the Vice President of Europe. The European division represented about 80 per cent of the international division. Alden felt that he reported directly to the President but cooperated with Tom's mission, which was seen as a staff function. During a meeting Tom would frequently try to assert his seniority by contradicting Alden, compared Europe unfavourably to other countries under his umbrella and provided relevant information about corporate policy which he had withheld from Alden.

Group solution: There were endless corridor meetings, sub-groupings and lobbying along with heated discussions between Tom and Alden which always ended in promises of continued commitment to mutual support and respect, but there was no long-term change.

Preferred solution: This issue of co-leadership needed to be confronted so that the lines of responsibility could be clearly demarcated. Had they discussed the game they would have seen that the source of their problem was David Hawksford, the President, whose style of management was to 'divide and conquer'.

In sum

If organisations are to be effective there's no use people sitting with group dynamic knowledge in their heads blaming everyone else for not applying it. If cultures are to change each individual who holds the desired values and attitudes has to assume the responsibility to take the risk of crossing their Rubicons every day and living by their values, however uncomfortable that may feel. In order to do this individuals have to confront their fears, make difficult choices and have the courage to be themselves.

Until these process issues are not only recognised but raised and dealt with, they will continue to influence the progress, tone and outcome of meetings, and the execution of the decisions made in them.

8 How does Company Politics Start?

> *It is a curious psychological fact that the man who seems to be egotistic is not suffering from too much ego but from too little.*
>
> (*Sydney J. Harris*)

How does company politics start?

How does a company culture become as disparate, negative and unfocused as many of us can contest they are? In a start-up operation, it is clear that individuals meet their own personal goals by optimising the realisation of the company's goals. By pleasing customers, making sales, working as a team with an 'all hands on deck' approach and getting it 'right first time', the company will grow successfully and with it their jobs, pay packets and status. Because of the small numbers, everyone is exposed and, if they want to be accepted by their peers, will be keen to work with the desired attitudes, values and behaviours. The only behavioural norms are *positive norms*. The culture would, therefore, be described as an 'excellent culture'.

Yet it is vital to remember that it is not merely the job, pay packet, status or exposure that motivates the staff. You probably know people (and may have done so yourself) who have left an organisation to go for a job with less money and lower status in order to regain both the thrill of working in a *team that is on their side* and the feeling of competence and self-worth that comes with successful achievement of goals.

As the company develops, the link between personal goals and objectives and those of the company is nothing like as clear. In addition, the leader who was once seen as warm, approachable and as much a part of each successful transaction as any other team member is now seen as critical, withdrawn and obstructive. How does this happen?

The need for power and control

By the time the company has reached about 30 employees, the decision to have functional managers is made. Now we are into the problem of *ego management* with its issues of *personal power and control.* Certain managers may feel insecure enough to insist that the leader no longer talks directly to his members of staff since this would interfere with the managers own authority. His feelings of competence and self-worth no longer come from achievement in a company-wide team. They now come from the recognition of his departments achievements and so he becomes *territorial, divisive and closed.*

Excluding the leader solves the insecure manager's need for power and control but now the leader feels out of control. He begins to insist, therefore, on tighter and tighter systems and procedures in order to retain control, since this has become his only source of information. The manager won't always agree with the leader's decisions on these systems. Although he does not mention this at meetings, for fear of conflict and reprisals (since he has a need for approval and recognition like everyone else), he *will* convey it to his staff, one way or another. He may even go down to them and say: 'You won't believe what he wants now. Another system! Well, I'm not doing it'.

As a result of the managers interventions the staff begin to view the leader as a selfish autocrat who doesn't trust them, like them and, since he never speaks to them, cannot understand their problems. They, too, have a need for recognition and one of the ego defence mechanisms generally used when individuals feel distrusted, disliked and misunderstood is 'projection' and so they distrust, dislike and misunderstand *him.* On the rare occasions that the MD or CEO does walk around the office, it is this dislike and suspicion that he sees in their eyes and this is extremely uncomfortable since he, too, has a need for recognition and approval.

In order to protect himself from feeling discomfort, the MD begins to shut the door of his office, and stay in it longer. This is interpreted as proof that he doesn't care about his employees or the business. Now when he plucks up the courage to venture forth, the eyes show not just dislike but resentment and anger. So now he stays away from the office. Next round he sees not only resentment and anger but indifference since they have now given up on him altogether. So he starts to get on a plane and stay out of the country or become involved in activities external to the business where he *does* get approval and recognition. Rather than be inwardly-looking as he was at the inception of the company, he is now outwardly-looking which would be fine if he was the chairman, but the employees, because of their misplaced dependence on authority, look to the CEO and MD for strong leadership.

Individuals cannot focus on achieving organisational goals when their overwhelming concern is with meeting their ego defensive needs. Their need for approval and recognition encourages them to suppress their true feelings and thoughts in the hope of pleasing others and deal with disagreements with fight or flight behaviour instead – aggression, manipulation or avoidance – which are the basis of company politics as Chapter 7 demonstrated. Paradoxically this results in their getting even less approval and less recognition.

Competition and culture

It can be seen, then, that as the organisation increases in size, one of the major blocks to progress is the *competition* between certain top team members and mirrored by their staff, in an attempt to hang onto feelings of power and control by promoting and defending personal or departmental goals above those of the organisation.

Hence, in a typical team meeting in an attempt to self-image actualise, members:

1 Ignore the proposals of others
2 Keep quiet for fear being made to look foolish
3 Say yes when they mean no
4 Interrupt each other to introduce their own idea
5 Get into 'win–lose' shouting matches
6 Accommodate in the meeting and sabotage outside
7 Raise issues in corridor meetings at the coffee machine rather than in the real meeting
8 Make team decisions in the absence of some members
9 Form 'partnerships' or 'power blocks' to support one idea against another
10 Use eye-contact to share disbelief and conspire against a decision whilst saying nothing
11 Take silence as agreement, when it invariably means precisely the opposite.

Battles rage discreetly or otherwise between individuals, but it's very difficult to summon up the courage to raise the reasons for them. After such experiences some team members metaphorically or literally put agreed plans in drawers and don't implement them whilst others will implement their variation which, after clever interpretation, meets their personal values, goals and agenda!

When they return to the follow-up meeting and find some have and some have not done what they thought was agreed, the level of anger, frustration, distrust and disrespect increases and is carried forward into the current discussion. Hence team behaviour becomes characterised by individuals defending their position and self-esteem, rather than supporting a group decision for the good of the company.

Before individuals attempt to change their behaviour, it is appropriate to ask:

- Why do individuals self image-actualise rather than self-actualise?
- Why do they need recognition?
- Why do they become ego-defensive?
- How did they develop this need to please others?

The need for recognition

From an early age individuals are taught to perceive their world in a certain way – not their way but the way adults view things: there is a 'right' way and a 'wrong' way. Their behaviour is constantly compared to some model out there that is perfect: a brother, a sister, a class mate, a fantasy in the mind of the adult authority. What they are not aware of is that the adults that they live with have different views of the truth from the adults living next door and that one teacher has a different model of a 'good child' from another.

Because *their* adults are convinced they are right, when children make mistakes in their eyes they are made to feel not quite good enough, never fully acceptable, slightly inadequate. Rather than see mistakes as an opportunity to learn the right way to do things they begin to dread them and grow up with the irrational belief (Ellis, 1971) that *making mistakes is terrible*. In addition, when they make mistakes and are not, in other words, perfect, the disapproval and rejection they receive makes them feel awful. The only way to feel good is to get people to love them and approve of them. Thus, they also grow up with a second irrational belief that *people must love me or I'll be miserable* (Ellis, 1971), and that to win love they must conform to others' expectations.

In adulthood, because of these authority issues developed as a child, when people stick their neck out and do things their way, if others see it as a mistake, they convince themselves that the other's judgement is justified, and that they themselves must be wrong.

Irrational beliefs are 'irrational' because people are bound to make mistakes, especially if they're trying out new things in their attempt to develop new skills, new methods and paths for the organisation, and because it is inevitable that not everyone will love them. People's opinions of them and what's right and wrong are partly their own responsibility, but partly also the responsibility of the other person. They are based not only their own behaviour but on the other person's expectations because – they like everyone else – have their own authority issues about what's right and wrong and how others *should behave.*

So, at a very early age they develop the need to be 'perfect', and their concept of 'perfect' is defined outside of themselves by authorities on the subject. Further, their need to be 'perfect' is tied up with the two irrational beliefs, 'making mistakes is terrible' and 'people must love me or I'll be miserable', as shown in Figure 12.

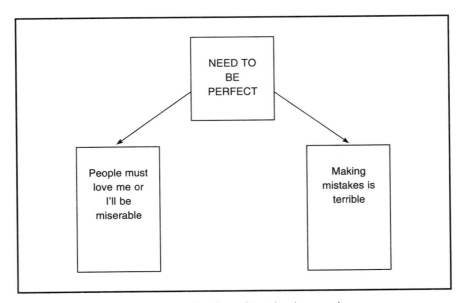

Figure 12   Our fear of 'getting it wrong'

Ego-defence mechanisms

As they learn of some 'perfect' being to whom they're supposed to aspire and how painful making mistakes and getting it wrong can be, in terms of loss of face and love, people lose confidence and in order to prevent others discovering their faults they develop *ego-defence mechanisms*.

People defend their ego by distorting or denying a reality that would otherwise arouse anxiety. Individuals use defence mechanisms all the time and they are effective up to a point:

> *Pros*: Defence mechanisms serve the invaluable function of allowing people to get on with the business of living their lives without surfacing feelings such as guilt and inadequacy and experiencing the anxiety caused by these.
>
> *Cons*: The more they turn away from anxiety-provoking realities, the less in touch people are with reality and the less they're able to deal with it constructively. When they use defence mechanisms to suppress or redirect onto others their problems with themselves, then they sabotage everyone including themselves.

The following are some common defence mechanisms:

> - *Rationalisation* – Deceiving yourself and others by giving socially acceptable reasons to justify doing, or planning to do, something for unconscious or unacceptable reasons. This is one of the most common defences. (*'There's no point in doing a good job, no one will notice.'*)
> - *Denial* – Refusing to be objective so as to avoid anxiety. (*'Don't worry. We've done enough preparation. It'll be all right on the night.'*)
> - *Projection* – Seeing in others the things about yourself that you don't wish to acknowledge, e.g. seeing someone as arrogant and controlling whilst behaving towards them in an arrogant and controlling manner, thereby converting an internal threat into an external one.
> - *Blaming* – Blaming others or the situation for your own problems: for example, after being found to have done a bad

job, you find someone else to blame. (*'Of course I couldn't make the sale, we don't have a marketing strategy.'*)

- *Intellectualisation* – Cutting yourself off from your feelings by dealing with them with on an intellectual level. (*'Yes, the culture causes me considerable distress. Employees find it difficult to endure a demoralised atmosphere, let alone the constant non-cooperation from the sales department and that, in combination with the lack of respect from their managers, eventually gets to them.'*)
- *Displacement* – Being afraid to express or even experience feelings against whoever has aroused them. The person first represses them and then releases them on a safer object. (*When subjected to humiliation and various defeats throughout the day, we may jump down the throat of a subordinate or friendly colleague.*)

These are some of the ego-defence mechanisms individuals use to avoid admitting to themselves or others that they are wrong, that they are not perfect. These are the 'fight' or 'flight' behaviours that neither help individuals grow nor encourage others to help them grow, as shown in Figure 13.

The need to seem 'perfect' and win approval by conforming to some external given of what is right and wrong, some truth, may mean that rather than experiment with change and risk the inevitable mistakes, individuals are either:

1   *Dependent* – i.e. keep their heads down, wont take risks, stay uncreatively conforming, don't question or seek others opinions

or

2   *Counterdependent* – i.e. encourage closed communications and behave uncooperatively and competitively

Rather than

3   *Interdependent* – i.e. open, collaborative, creative, objective and authentic.

One of the crucial steps to individuals acting in the attempt to self-actualise rather than self-image actualise is to understand their authority issues, so that they can assert their own beliefs and values and receive other beliefs and values without becoming ego-defensive.

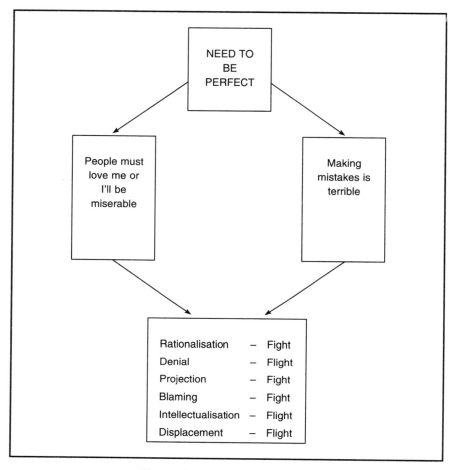

Figure 13   Hiding our 'mistakes'

Issues with authority

Dependents and counterdependents, unlike interdependents, have problems with authority in that they are trapped in a rigid response:

1   *Dependents* believe that they *always* have to do the approved thing, so that they can gain approval.
2   *Counterdependents* believe they *always* have *not* to do the approved thing, so that they can be 'free'.

> 3   *Interdependents* believe that each situation can be *objectively assessed* on its own merits so that they can seek advice or reassurance when they need it and get on with their job when they don't.

Dependents and counterdependents are inclined to be overly suspicious, guarded and thin-skinned and surprisingly have in common a tendency to be acutely sensitive to the possibility of *criticism, rejection or disapproval.*

(a)   The dependent type

Dependents lack self-confidence and self-reliance and they passively allow others to assume responsibility for deciding when to complete a task, how to do a task and so on. They have difficulty initiating any activities on their own. They agree with others even when they know they are wrong. They are unable to make demands on others and put their own needs second so as to ensure that they do not destroy existing relationships.

Some dependents are tolerant up to the point where they feel pushed around. Then they sabotage through passive–aggressive tactics such as saying yes and meaning no, working slower than necessary or absenting themselves at crucial times. At this point they become counterdependent.

If dependent types have been brought up with the right values they strive for organisational goals since this will satisfy their personal goals, i.e. to get it 'right' and so they look fine to the customer. The problem is theirs, therefore, in the existential sense not the company's in the customer-care sense! However, because they are motivated by pleasing authority, if they keep their heads down in the attempt to win approval, their creative potential will remain untapped and it is this that needs to change if the organisation is to benefit from their input.

(b)   The counterdependent type

Counterdependents are superficially charming and manipulate others for personal gain. Their seemingly positive feelings for others are often an act. Some have little or no sense of shame and this lack of negative emotions may make it impossible for them to learn from their mistakes. Some lack positive emotions, which leads them to behave irresponsibly towards others.

They are suspicious of people and frequently angry and hostile. They expect to be mistreated or exploited by others and may read hidden messages into events. This is a projection of their own. Such individuals are reluctant to confide in others, bear grudges, and tend to blame others even when they themselves are at fault. Some show their irresponsible behaviour by working inconsistently, lying, and being impulsive, failing to plan ahead. Counterdependents are intolerant of tolerant individuals and see them as wet or weak. They become aggressive or passive – aggressive because they fear criticism, rejection or disapproval.

They have an ego-first mentality rather than a customer-first mentality. They thus put their personal goals and needs above those of the organisation. They do not think they have a problem, which is why you do! They are motivated by being difficult with authority, using their substantial energy and creativity to compete inside rather than outside the organisation, and it is this that needs to change

(c)   The interdependent type

Interdependents have self-confidence, self-reliance and assume responsibility for decisions. They initiate activities on their own. They are more likely to assert their own opinion and disagree with others. They are able to make demands on others but equally are willing to subordinate their own needs to ensure collaboration and to maintain working relationships. They are just as comfortable forming close relationships as they are with their own company.

They feel centred and have the positive attitudes, values and beliefs required by the organisation. These are much easier to keep and bring on board because they are self-starters when it comes to getting the job done. They are motivated by pleasing themselves by achieving the company goals. The main problem is that interdependents do not act when it comes to confronting counterdependents and dependents behaving counterdependently. Then they back off. Neither of these behaviour patterns was in their childhood experience, and so they didn't learn how to deal with it. They feel uncomfortable dealing with those who are into 'win–lose' aggression and competition rather than 'win–win' assertion and collaboration.

So, while interdependents don't have a significant problem with authority, they do have a problem with people who have a problem with authority. This is *their* authority issue. For fear of criticism, rejection or disapproval, they keep their heads down, avoid conflict and leave physically or psychologically or become aggressive, and this is where they need to change. At this point they are no longer interdependent but instead shift into one of the other two modes.

Followers' ambivalence about leaders

Because of the deep-seated authority issues of dependents, counter-dependents and interdependents, games will continue to be played no matter what the climate. In fact, it has nothing to do with the climate. These are personal ways of relating to authority which invariably means that whatever the leader does, whatever type of climate he attempts to create, he or she will never get it right. One typical example is that when the leader asks for opinions the staff say: 'He's the leader. Can't he make the decision?' and when he makes a decision they say: 'He's such an autocrat. He never asks our opinion.' This constant ambivalence about correct leadership behaviour is one way that we *rationalise* our own failure to act, as illustrated in Table 6.

Leaders' ambivalence about followers

Management have the same problem but in reverse: look at Table 7.

Internal rules about authority – the double bind

This *double bind* that followers and leaders find themselves in is an authority issue that has to be surfaced. Instead, what generally happens is that, after several attempts at pleasing others, the leader gives up and reverts to distant autocracy and autonomous decision-making, whilst the followers give up and revert to silent suspicion and sabotage. We give up because We've seen it, done it, been there and worn the tee-shirt. This may feel more comfortable in the short term but allowing the morale of the entire company to plummet, and with it the profits, will be a lot more uncomfortable in the long term.

Table 6 Followers' ambivalence about leaders

Leaders' behaviour	Employees' response
When their job is described in immense detail and they're required to follow explicit rules	'We're just robots. We're not allowed to show initiative'
When they're given the freedom to achieve their objectives in their own way	'The management never gives us any direction – how are we supposed to know what they want us to do?'
When they're asked to maintain data bases, complete reports, forms, time sheets, etc.	'It's a waste of time – no one uses or reads this information'
When there are no information systems in place	'How do they expect us to do our jobs when nothing gets recorded?'
When they don't have PCs on their desks	'How are we supposed to compete without up-to-date technology?'
When they're given PCs	'I'm not using one of these – I prefer the old system'
When they have annual review	'How am I supposed to know what went wrong 9 months ago? – if they'd told me at the time I could have improved by now'
When they have quarterly reviews	'Why am I always being reviewed. Why can't I just get on with my job?'
When a company meeting is arranged to inform everyone.	'What a waste of time and money – couldn't they send a memo or e-mail?'
When a memo or e-mail is sent	'I haven't got time to read all this bumph; they never speak to us face to face – can't they just tell us?'
When there is no Christmas party arranged	'I work hard all year for this company – the least they can do is show me and my partner how much they appreciate the time I put in'
When a Christmas party is organised.	'I'm not wasting my time going – I see enough of everyone all year round.'

Table 7 Leaders' ambivalence about followers

Employees' behaviour	Management response
When subordinates are cautious and detail conscious	'Can't they think for themselves?'
When subordinates show initiative	'They never tell me where they are or what they are doing'
When subordinates maintain data bases, complete reports, forms, time sheets, etc.	'I wish they'd stop wasting their time and focus on getting more business'
When they focus on getting more business and there are no systems in place.	'They never keep records – how can I manage the business?'

The double bind is the result of certain unstated rules about authority. The following has been developed from the work of Houston (1984):

(a)   Dependent team members

Unstated rules:

Member		Leader
I feel dependent		You are totally dependable
I feel ignorant		You know everything
I feel powerless	THEREFORE	You are omnipotent
I need affection		Only yours is good enough
I need approval		You must give it

Small print contract:

I will hang on your every word if you are there for me in every way that I demand. I will agree with you, support you and defer to you if you live up to my impossible expectations.

   If you do not come up to scratch and satisfy all my needs, wants and wishes, I will sulk, avoid eye contact and attempt to generally make you feel bad until you perform the godlike role I expect from you. I will continue to withhold myself until you perform, beg for forgiveness or leave.

Signed A dependent team member

Leaders complementary rules:

Member		Leader
You feel dependent		I shall be totally dependable
You need approval	THEREFORE	I shall withhold any disapproval I feel
You need approval		I shall be totally dependable

Small print contract:

I will do my utmost to be perfect. I expect it, you expect it, what else would I be? When I fail, which I am bound to do, I will assume that your rejection of me is justified but will conceal this in an attempt to be stronger, more dependable, more likeable, more all-knowing until I finally crack under the strain, give up on you or leave.

Signed Your omnipotent leader

(b)   Counterdependent team member

Unstated rules

Member		Leader
I feel dependent		You must not know my weakness
I feel ignorant		You're ignorant too
I feel powerless	THEREFORE	I won't allow you any power
I need affection		I'll not spare you any
I need approval		I'll keep disapproving until I get over it

Small print contract:

Nothing you can do or say will be good enough for me. If you include me in discussions I will complain that you haven't the guts to make autonomous decisions. If you make autonomous decisions I will complain that you never ask my opinion. If you try and get close I will laugh at your pathetic attempts to be friends. If you are distant and autocratic I will resent the way you put yourself above me. I will make sure that you feel at least as bad if not worse than I feel inside.

Signed A counterdependent team member

Leader's complementary rules:

Member	Leader
You act as if I'm stupid	I'll treat you with contempt
THEREFORE	
You disapprove of me	Therefore I'll disapprove of you

Small print contract:

I will attempt to gain your approval since I feel I should be able to gain everyones approval but if I continually fail I will have my eye on you. I will make sure I give as good as I get until one day you will be out. The last thing I will do is to attempt to understand you better since you are apparently as clear as glass to me. A difficult and conceited idiot.

Signed Your belligerent leader

As a leader or team member it is up to you to decide how far you will go along with people's expectations, how far you will react to them in your own defensive way and how far you will see your work as being to let them see what their *authority issues* and their *expectations* are, and how they affect the group dynamics of the company, its culture and productivity.

Authority issues in groups

The following are some examples of how these *different orientations towards authority* contribute to the company politics within the groups.

(a)   Autocratic leadership

If the leader comes over as rather autocratic at times, reactions from members will vary. Some people enjoy being told what to do or think, and a relationship rather similar to that between a parent and child is maintained in an immature way between two adults, thus allowing little chance for personal and career development. Some people do not enjoy being told what to do or think, maybe because they are too autocratic by nature. Rebellions against the leadership will almost surely develop, subgroups develop and pre- and post-corridor meetings take place where people lobby for support, Many of the ultimate decisions are made outside the meeting when the leader feels less threatened and therefore prepared to listen to alternative viewpoints. Most people fall somewhere between these two extremes, and may find themselves alternating in feelings about the leadership:

John Scully

The President of a corporation, John Scully, was so autocratic during meetings that he would announce a policy that was clearly flawed but refused to compromise. For example, he decided that normal coffee was bad for the company and therefore instructed the suppliers only to supply decaffeinated coffee for all the machines. There were two subgroups, one group of Vice Presidents objected strongly and said it was not what people wanted and the other group said they had better things to discuss. John ignored them both.

Group solution: All the Vice Presidents gave up on John and sabotaged his decision after the meeting. As a result of the bad feelings aroused by not being listened to they and their staff agreed to persuade the supplier to put normal coffee in decaffeinated tins. This is a funny example, but it was repeated time and time again over business strategy, technical development, financial issues and so on.

Preferred solution: John needed to recognise that his decisions were constantly sabotaged, and ask the Vice Presidents what it was about for them. They needed to raise the issues of his autocratic behaviour and how what seemed to them to be irrational decisions were being sabotaged by their dependent behaviour in meetings and their counterdependent behaviour outside them. The decision-making process needed to be the centre of the discussion and how this group will make decisions in future (e.g. consensus, majority vote, decision by vocal minority, decision by by-passing, decision by authority and so on).

(b)   Fight for power and control

When chairing a meeting it is not uncommon to find that someone will try and make the chair look incompetent, others will wait for him to put that person in his place, others may try and defend him and others compete with him. All these are bids for power and control. Some want the chairman to take it, some want a group member to take it, some want to be the group member who takes it. If someone has set himself up as a leader, then you can be sure that someone else will want to knock him down.

If the leader is not aware that individuals are projecting their authority issues onto him he might take it personally and succumb to the pressure. If he understands that these bids for leadership are inevitable he can raise the issue as one of power and control and the team can deal with it out in the open and move on. If the bids are ignored members of the group will begin to take sides and the real purpose of the group will be in danger of being forgotten:

Wolfgang Schmidt

In a residential top team development workshop in Germany, the management team were asked to do a presentation. As the technical manager, Wolfgang Schmidt, was presenting his views, the sales manager, Hans Reinhold rearranged the seating, moved tables and generally ignored him.

Actual solution: Everyone, including Wolfgang, pretended it wasn't happening knowing that this game had been played many times before with detrimental effects on the outcome of meetings.

Preferred solution: Anyone in the group could have said: I feel uncomfortable that you, Hans, are moving furniture while Wolfgang is speaking. Hans would sit down and look amused yet sheepish. Then add: 'This isn't the first time we've done this to each other is it? This is an example of the disrespect we have for each others' views in this team.' Counterdependency on Wolfgang's part, dependency on the part of those who deferred and the lack of interdependent behaviour by those waiting for the leader to confront him are the issues that could be raised as typical team behaviour.

(c)   Pairing

Many teams suffer from two or more people who always support each other, never disagree, round up on other members of the group, sit together, exchange looks, nods, winks or whisper confidences. When this happens the rest of the team feel left out, powerless, lack confidence and feel jealous. As a result other pairing can start and hence create factions in the team. Either that or the opposite occurs when two proponents never support each other, always disagree, lobby for the support of other members and look daggers at each other. When this happens the rest of the team feel uncomfortable, frustrated and angry.

If pairing is ignored, neither the team nor individual needs will be satisfied, chances are individuals will dread team meetings and the task will suffer. It is essential to raise the issue, help all members to take responsibility for it, look for reasons and discuss it's effects.

Tom Lundberg and Raymond Vowler

Tom Lundberg and Raymond Vowler would join forces to outmanoeuvre Ed Smethers, the domestic Vice President of sales and marketing, who was trying to get control of international sales and have Tom fired. Because of the pairing he tended to capitulate during meetings, which affected the quality of decisions made.

Actual solution: Everyone recognised what was taking place, but it was ignored in the meeting.

Preferred solution: Someone needed to raise Ed's hidden agenda and the response by Tom and Raymond to it. Their counterdependent aggression and his passive dependent behaviour in capitulating to it meant that almost every organisational plan was coloured by this underlying conflict. Until these process issues are raised, task needs will not be met.

Process review isn't easy

In some respects the content of the meeting can be seen as a backdrop for group members to learn about their dependence, counterdependence or interdependence on authority. From this experience, they can stop relying on or blaming the management and others and begin to take responsibility *themselves* for what is going on in the organisation.

Once everyone has understood and owned their own ambivalence regarding authority it is difficult to continue corridor meetings on the topic. The leader's role is not to try and be what others want him to be but to help himself and others understand the authority issues that cause sabotage and block progress.

The leader becomes a screen on which each member may *project* his own particular manner of relating to authority. Managers who are prepared to allow this are taking a risk as they may reflect back their own authority issues and make the situation worse by becoming defensive and autocratic. So, before dealing with the authority issues in the group, individuals first need to deal with their *own authority issues*.

In sum

The resolution of authority issues in groups is key to the effective functioning of group members. To cross Rubicons, be authentic and confront company politics individuals must:

1   Abandon their belief in authority and one truth
2   Accept responsibility for their own behaviour
3   Stop self-image actualising
4   Stop catastrophising
5   Stop daydreaming
6   Act on their decisions.

In Chapters 9–14 the skills and techniques that individuals need to stay interdependent, remain objective and raise the real issues will be discussed.

9 The Phenomenological Approach and Action

The Gestalt Prayer:

'I do my thing, and you do your thing,
I am not in this world to live up to your expectations
And you are not in this world to live up to mine.
You are you, and I am I,
And if by chance, we find each other, it's beautiful.
If not, it can't be helped.'

(*Fritz Perls*)

Abandoning belief in authority and truth

Individuals frequently hold back from asserting their own opinion and contradicting those of others, because they are afraid of getting it wrong and not being liked, as was noted in the Chapter 8. If the organisation is to use the potential of all the people in it, individuals have to stop this self-image actualising. One step in this direction is to confront the fantasy that there is a 'right' answer, that there is an authority that holds the monopoly on what is the 'truth' or 'perfect'. There has never been a truth, there will never be a truth and reminding themselves can help individuals take the risk of saying what they believe.

Even science is, in effect, merely a democracy wherein if enough people vote for a fact it must be true. The majority of people believed the 'fact' that the earth was flat until it was 'proved' that it was round, when the majority of people believed the 'fact' that it was round until it was 'proved' that it was an oblate spheroid and now the majority of people believe that to be 'fact'. Until someone discovers another 'truth'!

Similarly Newton 'proved' the fact that time was absolute and this was believed by a majority of people until Albert Michelson raised the question, that Einstein answered, that Time was in fact relative. Similarly, our faith in Einstein's concept of constant change within order and stability is being rocked by Chaos Theory with its belief in permanent instability.

A topical example is that of BSE. If you're a farmer you will have a different view of the facts than if you're a consumer, if you're a Tory politician you have a different view of the facts than if you're a German politician, and if you're a scientist with all the relevant data you'll interpret the facts differently from another scientist with all the data!

There is no truth, there is no right or wrong. There are only people's opinions, interpretations and perceptions based on their past experience, knowledge and feelings at the time. This is the *phenomenological approach* that all knowledge is subjective and therefore cannot be considered apart from the mind doing the 'knowing'. Individuals merely select the evidence that fits their own theoretical basis. Dependents choose to believe that other people hold the truth and follow their lead whilst counter-dependents believe that they hold the truth and demand that others follow theirs; the truth in fact will depend on each individual's preconceived ideas.

Have you ever been to a film and taken from it a very definite message which seems meaningful and obvious? As you walk out in absorbed, stunned silence, the individual you are with starts to describe a totally different and, to you, banal message. Isn't it incredibly annoying? But who is right? What do you see when you look at Figure 14?

Figure 14 An ambiguous picture

Did you see a young woman or an old woman? Look at Figure 14 until you see both. When you saw the Young Woman were you 'right'? When you saw the Old Woman were you 'right'? No, they were just different points of view. What influence did reading the word 'young' or 'old' have the second time you looked at Figure 14?

The perception of each individual is the result of their perspective based on *past experience* and the way they *feel* at the time.

> ⁶Over time our individual perceptions settle down to give us our personal view of the world. That is how we see the world . . . in which we live and act. That world may be full of inadequacies, prejudices, stereotypes and confusions. That is the only world we have⁹ (*de Bono, 1996, p. 31*)

Gestalt psychologists used illusions to illustrate that individuals do not passively respond to stimulus but that everyone interprets input in their own ways. Look at Figure 15. Which line do you see as the longer of the two?

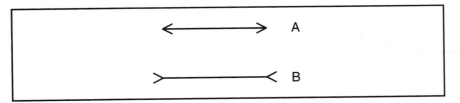

Figure 15 The Müller–Lyer Illusion

Whether you know this illusion or not, it's very difficult, if not impossible, not to see *B* as the longer line. The fact is, they are identical. If we passively responded to data we would see them as the same. As the Gestaltists say: 'The whole is more than the sum of the parts.' As de Bono (1996, p. 28) puts it:

> ⁶We live in the world we 'see'. But the world we see is not the world around us but the perceived world in our minds. The physical world may be exactly the same but different people will see different things.⁹

Each individual's understanding of their world does not come from outside themselves but from their interpretation of the event, and it's that interpretation that's all there is. There is no truth. External reality 'is not something objective and real but something subjective and ideal'. (Kant, 1881). For existentialists, there is no meaning outside or independent of what we make of it. In other words:

> The reality is there is no reality.

Active participants in the 'truth'

Perceiving is an *active process* involving *selection* and *interpretation* of an event in line with each individual's personal beliefs which the following situation illustrates:

> 'A man stood before the mirror and combed his hair. He checked his face carefully for any places he might have missed shaving and then put on the conservative tie he had decided to wear. At breakfast, he studied the newspaper carefully, and over coffee, discussed the possibility of buying a new washing machine with his wife. Then he made several phone calls. As he was leaving the house he thought about the fact that his children would probably want to go to that private camp again this summer. When the car didn't start, he got out, slammed the door and walked down to the bus stop in a very angry mood. Now he would be late.'
>
> *(Bransford and Johnson, 1973, p. 145)*

Now re-read the passage using the word 'Stockbroker' in the place of the word 'man'. Now read the passage once more putting the word 'Unemployed' in front of the word 'man'. How did your perception of the events change? What kind of newspapers were they reading? Which section? What tone did the discussion about the new washing machine have? What type of car did each get into?

Since perceptions of the same event differ as a result of past experience and the feelings at the time, the opinions, views and expectations of others, including those in 'authority', can be viewed as simply *'hypotheses'* which are no better or worse than each other.

'You are you and I am I'

So, there is no right or wrong out there, only what individuals make of it. They are responsible for their own life experience, how they view it, and what they do with it. In other words there is:

> No perfect, no truth, no authority, only opinion.

Individuals in organisations cannot continue to live their lives trying to live up to other people's expectations if they are to take the risk of voicing their opinion. Everyone has had different experiences and others' expectations are not right or wrong, they are simply their expectations. Your perfect is not my perfect.

An example I used to use when Margaret Thatcher was in power was that, in her role of Prime Minister, she was loved by many because she appeared to be a dogmatic, intelligent woman and hated by many because she appeared to be a dogmatic, intelligent woman. If she had decided to stay at home and be a housewife those who loved her would hate her and those that hated her would love her. You have to be true to yourself: you can never get it right in some people's 'eyes'.

Don't procrastinate!

Having an approach to life that does not expect perfect 'right–wrong' solutions can help individuals to stop procrastinating and cross their Rubicons whereas attempting to be perfect can result in individuals putting things off until tomorrow.

For example, a friend of mine was telling me how hard she was finding the thought of visiting a friend of hers who was dying of cancer. My friend is a trained counsellor, studying Buddhism, is reading the Tibetan Book of Living and Dying and feels she 'should' therefore be perfect at dealing with this situation. She 'ought' to get it right and 'must' be in control and skilled at all times. This is her self-concept and her need for *self*-recognition comes from this behaviour as well as her need for recognition from others. She was putting off the visit until she could get it right. But there are no

> 'shoulds' 'oughts' and 'musts', there are only opinions. We discussed it and she decided that instead of waiting for perfection she would remember the inspiring words of Albert Ellis:
>
> • If a thing's worth doing it's worth doing badly!•

This can help move even the worst perfectionist to act. If individuals give themselves permission to do it badly they overcome the irrational fear of not being perfect, they act and by taking the pressure off themselves to perform they do in fact do a brilliant job. Or at least as brilliant a job as needed doing. The friend dying of cancer wanted a visit, not a perfect visit.

If individuals take the risk of confronting the saboteurs they will probably get more, not less, recognition for it. At the very least they'll be able to sleep at night because they are living by their own principles and expectations, not others'.

If they can accept that life is just a matter of opinion and that others' views of them or their work is at least 50 per cent their responsibility (since they are judging it from their point of view, expectations and upbringing), then they can begin to take the pressure off themselves to 'get it right'. That is, the pressure of trying to self-image actualise, to 'please all of the people all of the time' and put everyone first but themselves.

In sum

By believing that there is an authority that is right and by trying to conform, individuals lose faith in their own opinions, avoid taking the risk of being themselves, deny the organisation their input and suppress everything they have to offer.

Conventional culture change programmes try to create an environment where people feel free to use their own ideas, make decisions and act autonomously but they don't. By understanding that there are no 'right' answers, that there is no authority who knows best, that rather than please others, they would do better by the organisation to take responsibility for their own job, they no longer need to sit and wait for permission to act.

10   We Hypnotise Ourselves with Our Own Language

> ⁶Men are disturbed not by things, but by the views they take of them.⁹
>
> (*Epictetus, 100 AD*)

Accepting personal responsibility for behaviour

People differ in the extent to which they feel that they are responsible for their own behaviour. Rotter (1966) proposed the concept of *locus of control* to establish differences between individuals in this regard. He found that:

(a)   Those with *internal locus of control* have the perception that they are responsible for what happens to them
(b)   Those with *external locus of control* have the perception that luck, fate, other people or outside forces beyond their personal control determine their lives.

Locus of control is assessed by a self-administered questionnaire developed by Rotter comprising 23 pairs of opposed statements such as:

(a)   Promotions are earned through hard work and persistence
(b)   Making a lot of money is largely a matter of getting the right breaks.

(a)   In the long run people get the respect they deserve
(b)   Unfortunately people's worth often passes unrecognised no matter how hard they try.

(a)   The average person can have an influence on government decisions
(b)   This world is run by the few people in power, and there is not much the little guy can do about it.

Several hundred studies using Rotter's questionnaire have consistently found that:

- *Internals* tend to take responsibility for what happens to them, see the events of life as having a cause–effect relationship with themselves as the cause, be more independent, more achieving, more reliant on their own judgement and resistant to influence, more judgmental, more politically active, have a greater sense of personal power. They are more likely to delay instant gratification in order to achieve long-term goals and evaluate information on the basis of its merit rather than on the basis of the status or expertise of the source of the information.
- *Externals* are more likely to suffer feelings of inadequacy, anxiety, fatigue, confusion, depression. pointlessness, powerlessness, worthlessness, frustration and anger.

Since locus of control is a learned personality characteristic, probably highly dependent on cultural values, individuals can learn to develop a stronger sense of *internal control*. They can learn to take responsibility for their own feelings and do something about their predicament.

Hypnotising yourselves with your own language

To those individuals who are fed up with work yet feel powerless to change I often say:

‘You can do anything with your life. You can even change your name and move to California!’

(Yalom, 1980, p. 216)

Their reply is quite predictable. They say: ‘I *can't* do that. I've got a wife/husband and two kids to support.’ ‘Well,’ I say, ‘You can put the two kids in a Home and divorce your partner.’ To which everyone in the group laughs and the person responds confidently ‘I can't do *that*!’

Say ‘I *won't* do that,’ I reply, and after a little confusion, the person tries it: ‘I won't put my kids in a home and divorce my wife.’

It's remarkable how the atmosphere in the room changes as he and everyone else begins to realise that it is they themselves that keeps them where they are in life. It is, in fact, *their values* that are making them do things that they hate. Once the person realises that they *choose* to support the family they love, it makes getting up in the morning a lot easier.

Individuals *are* free to make changes to their lives. They are not as stuck as they think. They simply *hypnotise* themselves with their own language. Some of the examples I hear all the time are:

I can't use this system	*rather than*	I won't use this system
I can't complain to my manager	*rather than*	I won't complain to my manager
I can't confront my colleague	*rather than*	I won't confront my colleague
I can't solve my own interdepartmental issues	*rather than*	I won't solve my own interdepartmental issues.
I can't admit I need help	*rather than*	I won't admit I need help
I can't change	*rather than*	I won't change

One way to 'unstick' a company culture is to get everyone more and more aware of their freedom to choose how they act.

Taking responsibility for your own behaviour

Some still say: 'How can I be responsible for my own behaviour when other people in the organisation are what block it?' But the real question is: 'How can other people be responsible for *your* behaviour?' What a cop out. If I were to ask them: 'What's stopping you act?' my hunch is that the answer would be: 'Other people who are not interested in achieving company goals.'

In other words, they're saying, 'I am not responsible for my own behaviour because when other people block me, they *cause* me to feel demotivated and dispirited and I therefore become passive.'

'What have you done about it?' I ask.
'Me? What can I do about it?' they reply, innocently.
'Who's pulling your strings?' I ask.
'Everyone else', is the triumphant reply.
My next question: 'Why do you give away your power so easily?' is
greeted with a blank face and the question:
'What do you mean?'

Most individuals imagine that a *situation causes their feelings* and
behaviour. They say that being stuck on the M25 made them angry and
drive carelessly, listening to music makes them feel sad and cry, overload
of work makes them stressed and panic-stricken. The situation causes
them to have a feeling which causes them to behave accordingly. Look at
Figure 16.

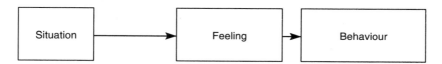

Individuals argue, for example, that others in the organisation who are
obstructive cause them to feel bad and give up

But does everyone feel bad and give up when confronted by people being
obstructive? The answer must surely be 'No'. Some people are
obstructive back, some try to influence them, some give up but don't
care.

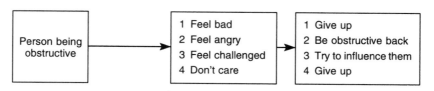

Figure 16   The relationship between a situation and the resulting feelings/behaviour

This confronts the premise that there's a causal relationship between a situation and the resultant feelings and behaviour, since there are four people responding to the same situation with four different feelings and behaviours.

Each of these four people must, therefore, be doing something else in between, in order for them to feel and act differently to the same situation. What is it that they are doing that's different? What is it that the person who feels bad and the person who feels challenged are doing in the middle box in Figure 17 that is different?

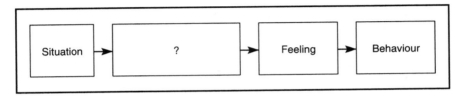

Figure 17   How does the situation lead to feelings/behaviour

We feel what we think

It's the way people *view* the situation, their *interpretation* of it or their *expectation* that causes their feelings and resultant behaviour, not the situation itself. Look at Figure 18.

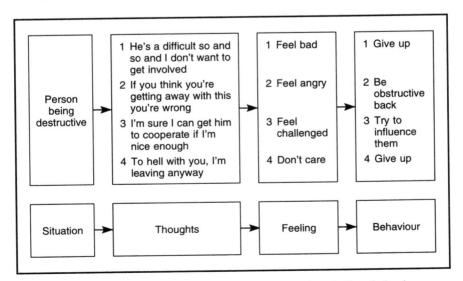

Figure 18   How do thoughts about a situation lead to feelings/behaviour

For example, an individual's boss tells him his work is inadequate:

- He can *choose* to feel *good* because he *thinks* his boss is an idiot and wouldn't know good work if he saw it.
- He can *choose* to feel *bad* because he *thinks* his boss is knowledgeable and he respects his opinion.
- He can *choose* to feel *indifferent* because he *knows* he's accepted a job elsewhere and the boss doesn't know it.
- He can *choose* to feel *frightened* because he *imagines* that this is the first step to getting dismissed.
- He can *choose* to feel *interested* because he *sees* it as a learning experience.

In order to change the way they feel about a situation and their resultant behaviour, individuals must change the *thoughts* (views, beliefs, interpretations) that they have about it (Ellis, 1971).They need to replace their *negative self-talk* with *positive self-talk*.

So in the example of a person being obstructive, in order to avoid feeling bad and giving up the first person may say to himself the sequence of things in Figure 19.

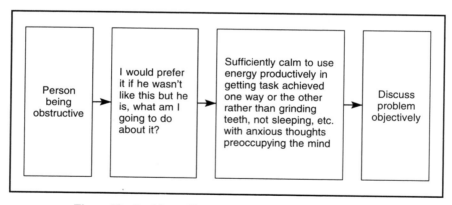

Figure 19   Positive self-talk and objective problem-solving

Taking responsibility for your own feelings

If individuals view things as a '*threat*' rather than a problem to be solved, their bodies automatically get into a '*fight–flight' response* and they feel anxious and behave by attacking or avoiding. But they do have a choice:

If, for example, I was sitting at this computer with an 18-month-old baby and a lion started to bound through the window, what would my automatic reaction be? Probably to run, freeze or (stupidly) fight. But an 18-month-old baby, seeing a huge fluffy cat coming through the window would try and cuddle it. The baby would not view it as a threat. If we went through life more like an 18-month-old rather than ourselves with all our learned fears, life would be a lot less stressful.

Now I know some of you are thinking: 'But an 18-month-old would go and play on the M25 and that's a real threat,' or 'Taking an overdose of coloured pills is a real threat but a child would do it.' Yes, OK, there are certain real threats in our life and the fact that we have an autonomic nervous system which produces the adrenaline we need to deal with it is great. But:

- Is a person being difficult in the organisation a threat or a problem to be solved?
- Is a weekly meeting that you dread a threat or a problem to be solved?
- Is the fact that you cannot get cooperation from an adjacent department a threat or a problem to be solved?
- Is the fact that you spend most of your time on customer sites and feel more likely to go to their Christmas party than your own a threat or a problem to be solved?

Individuals spend days, weeks, months winding themselves up because they will not confront issues as problems but instead view them as 'win–lose' situations where their catastrophic fantasies guarantee that they will be the one to lose:

Individuals need to either change their situation or the way they view it, but there's no point in living their lives staying in the same situation and continuing to view it with stress, horror or unhappiness.

Regaining power and control

However individuals are treated, whatever is said to them, no one can make them feel anything. Only they can make themselves feel by the way they *view* the situation, how they *interpret* what was said or done. This is a very powerful position to be in. Each individual is totally in control. That's not to say that others' opinions aren't worth listening to, but they are not pearls of wisdom either! If someone says they're stupid it doesn't make them stupid! They can begin with an attitude that gives them a 50 per cent chance of being right! Instead of jumping down their throat or avoiding them like the plague, they can view it as an *interesting hypothesis* and discuss, in an unemotional manner, what *specifically* they did or said that gives them that opinion.

By the end of the discussion they may agree that the other person is, in fact, 100 per cent right and they were acting or saying something stupid and thereby learn something. On the other hand, after due consideration, they may think that they are 100 per cent right and their behaviour was reasonable. At least they are now in a problem-solving, rather than 'win–lose' frame of mind and confronting issues rather than dealing with them in fight or flight.

In sum

1 Individuals are responsible for their own behaviour and are in control
2 They feel what they think and then act accordingly
3 If they control their thoughts, they can manage their feelings and behave more effectively
4 By doing so, they gain a greater control over the situations they find themselves in
5 They feel free to make choices which support their goals and objectives such as confronting company politics.

> So, a first step to 'taking responsibility for your own behaviour' in the existential sense is to accept that your behaviour is caused by things that go on *inside* your head rather than *outside* it!

Recognising that the way you respond to situations (thoughts, feelings, behaviours) is solely your responsibility, and that you can therefore choose to respond differently is a prerequisite to developing an *internal locus of control*. Controlling their thoughts helps individuals conserve energy and respond to the here and now rather than some fantasy about what they think might be happening. This is easier said than done because individuals are not always aware of their thoughts nor are they aware of the techniques that can be used to change them. Chapters 11–13 describe three such techniques.

_____ **Self-Analysis** _____

Taking responsibility for your own feelings

(a) Complete the following sentences regarding your feelings in each situation. Focus on how you *feel* rather than on your thoughts about the other person.

1   When someone dislikes me I feel . . . . . .
2   When someone is overdependent on me I feel . . . . . .
3   When someone talks about themselves all the time I feel . . . . . .
4   When someone is angry with me I feel . . . . . .
5   When someone is attracted to me I feel . . . . . .
6   When someone puts me down I feel . . . . . .
7   When someone breaks a confidence I feel . . . . . .
8   When someone is late for an appointment I feel . . . . . .
9   When I'm in a meeting with my manager I feel . . . . . .
10   When I'm in a meeting of peers I feel . . . . . .
11   When I walk into a group of strangers I feel . . . . . .
12   When someone listens and understands me I feel . . . . . .

(b) Do you have *conflicting* feelings in any situations? Why do you think that is?

(c) Try writing an *opposite* feeling to your original one. What needs to change for you to feel different about the same situation?

(d) Who or what is *responsible* for your feelings?

So who makes you feel powerless, demotivated, worthless, stuck, stressed?!

11 Confronting Politics – The Stress of Inaction – The Anxiety of Action

'On many people's tombstones you could write: born 1748, died 1772, buried 1798.' (*Benjamin Franklin*)

Stay in the 'here and now'

Catastrophic fantasies, negative self-talk and 'shoulds', 'oughts' and 'musts' are all value judgements, interpretations, opinions, predictions, and views. Because they are often visualisations of the worst possible scenario individuals respond with either 'fight' or 'flight'. Staying in the here and now helps individuals to be *more open, honest and decisive* and *encourages action*. What does 'staying in the here and now' mean? The following is a scenario that many of us are familiar with and illustrates the point:

> Imagine you've had an argument in the middle of the office with a colleague who is a well known saboteur. He was unpleasant and rude. You drive home grinding your teeth, beeping your horn, frustrated and angry, thinking to yourself: 'He shouldn't have spoken to me like that', 'I should have answered him stronger', 'Why did I make the mistake in the first place?', 'Whose fault was it, anyway?', 'I'm sure I delegated that job to someone else'. You arrive home having gone through four sets of traffic lights and not remembering any of them.
>
> As you go in through the front door your partner comes to greet you and you are quite brusque. The children come up to you and you push them off. You sit down to eat and eat very fast because all the time in your mind you are thinking: 'How could he speak to me like that?', 'Why did I let him get away with it?', 'What am I going to do tomorrow?', 'How can I face everybody?'. And because of this, you've now got indigestion. You sit in front of the television and watch it for two hours but you don't see much because all the time

the image of the argument is swimming in front of your eyes and the same thoughts are going through your head. Now you've got a cracking headache.

You finally go to bed. Since your partner wants to read, you pick up a book and start to read but you read the same paragraph four times and still can't remember what it says. So you put your book down. Your partner falls asleep and finally you drop off. Three o'clock in the morning, your eyes flash open, your heart rate is going like the clappers and off you go again: 'How dare he say that to me?', 'Why didn't I answer him back more aggressively?', 'I don't need to take that sort of thing from him', 'It wasn't my fault anyway', 'How am I going to face him in the morning'?, 'I'm going to walk in and tell him what I think'.

What is it that is stressing you? Is there anything in the bedroom that's stressing you at that moment? Is it the bedclothes, your partner, the ceiling? No. There is nothing that is actually happening in the here and now that's stressful. It's only your anxious thoughts. Your thoughts about the argument yesterday and how you're going to handle yourself tomorrow. In other words:

Anxiety is rehearsing for tomorrow and reliving the past – stay in the 'here and now'.

If you don't stay in the here and now by either doing something constructive at 3 o'clock in the morning or get some sleep, chances are you're wasting energy that could otherwise be used *solving the problem the following day*. By aggravating yourself with fantasies you end up tired, irritated and are likely to deal with the situation in your habitual conflict handling style be it aggressive, passive–aggressive or avoidance.

Three zones of awareness

How do individuals learn to 'stay in the here and now'? To do this, it is helpful to consider experience as consisting of *three areas of awareness*:

---

1   Internal reality
2   External reality
3   Fantasy.

Staying in the here and now means remaining in internal and external reality: consciously *not* fantasising.

(a)   Internal reality

Internal reality is anything experienced inside the body right now. An individual might say: 'I can feel my mouth is dry, I can feel my elbow resting on the table and my right knee has a slight pain in it, I can feel the cold Dictaphone in my right hand and a slight pressure across my eyes.' That is their internal reality. No-one can take that away from them. That is how they experience themselves right now.

(b)   External reality

External reality consists of awareness of the external world right here and now. They can say: 'I can see a bunch of red roses, there is a bright light shining from the ceiling, I can see a pot with coffee in it, I can see trees outside the window, they are moving.' If they were to say: 'They are moving in the wind,' that's a fantasy because Powergen could have put an enormous windmill in their next-door neighbour's garden to generate electricity. In other words, external reality only relates to what they can see, without interpretation.

(c)   Fantasy

Fantasy consists of interpretations, assumptions or opinions. So they might say: 'I can see Becky at the computer. She has a frown on her face'. If they say: 'She's looking worried,' that's a fantasy. She may simply be concentrating. Fantasies, then, are assumptions and interpretations of the world around us. They are thoughts that cannot exist in internal and external reality. For example, you're walking down the corridor and the boss walks past with a frown on his face and ignores you. You immediately interpret this as proof that he hates the report you gave him last week. You spend a dreadful day fantasising about this only to find out that he was preoccupied by some personal matter. Fantasies can be a very important part of life for a number of reasons. Individuals use fantasies to make plans about where to go on holiday, the profit they expect in the next 12 months, expansion into a new market sector and confronting a saboteur. Fantasy is also the basis of creative art and literature and so on which depends on fantasy and imagination. Fantasy can also be relaxing as when reminiscing about a good relationship, a happy holiday or a successful experience.

Fruitful and destructive fantasy

What distinguishes fruitful fantasy from destructive fantasy is that individuals *take strength or act on* the former whilst merely *aggravating themselves* with the latter. Fantasy is a waste of energy if you don't act on it. You book the holiday, achieve your business plan, you expand into the new market. You paint the picture or write the book. You give yourself space to reminisce and relax. You confront the saboteur:

Anne Adair recounted how she successfully used this technique while queuing to buy a train ticket for an important meeting in London. 10 people were in front of her. After 5 minutes of standing on the same spot, she began to think that the man at the window was writing his memoirs, not simply buying a ticket! Worrying (fantasising) about what the others at the meeting would say if she was late, her heart rate began to increase. She began to perspire and had an image of herself grabbing the man by the scruff of his neck and dragging him away from the window, screaming at him to stand aside while she bought her ticket. Catching herself aggravating herself, she asked if she intended to do what she had imagined. *Was she going to act out her fantasy?* The answer not surprisingly, was: 'No.' At this point, she said to herself: 'Okay, if I'm not going to do anything, relax. Get into the here and now. Stop fantasising about my boss's comments. I'm late. The acid remarks will come whether I worry or not. So the best thing for me to do is conserve my energy and not worry.'

She focused on internal and external reality: 'There is a newspaper stand next to me and I can see *The Times* newspaper. I can see a woman in front of me with a red hat on. I can feel myself take a deep breath and I am aware of the tension across my eyes. It is easing a little. . .' Rather than fantasising about the past or future, she was now able to use her energy to make a rational decision regarding the choices she had in the current situation. To finish her story, she got her ticket, caught the train and wasn't late for the meeting. She arrived relaxed with plenty of energy to use where it was appropriate – in the 'here and now' of the meeting. Even had she arrived late, she could either arrive late and frazzled or late and energetic – the decision was hers.

The problem is that many individuals are very talented at living in a fantasy world. They can spend weeks, months, even years, aggravating themselves over things that happened in the past and their plans to do something about their future. Living in the past and future is a never-ending *downward spiral*.

For example, you come to a meeting worrying about a report you neglected to prepare. Because you're worrying about it you miss information during the meeting and therefore go to the next meeting not having done something that was asked of you last time. So you worry about that and miss more information and so on. Wherever you are, if you're not there 100 per cent you're wasting energy on the past and future.

Liz Slater complained that when she was at work, she continually worried about her children and when she was with her children, she continually worried about work. Neither work nor the children benefited from her presence. She became more satisfied, as did everyone else, when she spent 100 per cent of her energy on the children when at home and 100 per cent of her energy on work when at the office.

How to stay in the 'here and now'

Next time you're in a traffic jam stacked over Heathrow or delayed on the train, aggravating yourself won't help. Worrying about what people will say when you get to your meeting is an utter waste of energy. Worrying will not make the traffic move, the plane land or the train restart. As you worry, physiological changes such as your heart rate increasing, breathing becoming shallow and muscle tension use energy that needs to be conserved for your performance at the meeting:

> Either say to yourself: 'Is there anything I can do about this situation?' If there is, do it. If there isn't, stop wasting energy and focus on internal and external reality. If you're in a car, for example say things like: 'I can feel the cold steering wheel against my hand. There is a red car in front of me. I can see a policeman waving his arms. I can see a pink car in the mirror. I can feel the seat against my legs and the pedals under my feet. I can feel my heart rate reducing. I am feeling calmer.' Every now and again, as your fantasies push their way into your consciousness, take a deep breath and replace them with the words: 'Nothing Matters.' Probably, as you go into internal and external reality, you'll find that you take a deep breath.

> This is because as soon as you begin to get into internal and external reality, you knock out the negative self-talk which reverses the physiological changes such as shallow breathing and you begin to relax.

Telling people to stop worrying doesn't help, but asking them to get into internal and external reality does. As you do this every day, you will begin to find that you catch yourself fantasising in the car, at a meeting, during a presentation, at your desk, at the airport, and will begin to have choices about whether you use the fantasy and act or stop wasting energy.

In sum

Margaret Smith

Margaret Smith has a member of staff, Owen Williams, whose favourite game is to wind her up by coming in late, taking a coffee and reading the newspaper when he knows she is frantic about a deadline. Instead of confronting him, Margaret has spent months worrying about his bad time management, how she's going to handle his next extended coffee break, what she should do when he opens the newspaper, how she's going to get the work completed in spite of him and why she didn't deal with him a long time ago. She worries week after week, month after month, her anxiety created by reliving the past and rehearsing the future, but she never resolves the problem. So the organisation has lost the energy of two people – one playing and one not confronting politics. Had Margaret known the technique she could have chosen to live in the here and now and change her situation and thereby be a productive member of the management team increasing productivity and revenue, rather than have her emotional energy and time wasted on an unproductive fantasy.

Staying in internal and external reality is a way of reminding yourself that *nothing matters*. In the whole scheme of things, in the whole world, individuals are just a speck of dust. Nothing matters. Someone once said to me: 'That's all very well but you can't stop worrying. I made myself ill because of a long drawn-out divorce which cost me a fortune.' Well the point is he could have had a long drawn-out divorce without being ill. The illness didn't make the divorce any shorter or cheaper. Staying in the here and now puts problems into the right perspective. Rather than opt out, worry or be angry you solve problems more rationally, more satisfactorily and you don't make yourself ill. Either make a decision and resolve to act on it or stop fantasising and stay in the here and now.

12 The Difference between *Self*-Actualising and Self-*Image* Actualising

> 'When two people meet there are really six people present. There is each man as he sees himself, each man as the other person sees him and each man as he really is.'
>
> (*William James*)

Preoccupation with ourself

When individuals are preoccupied with the impression they're making, with self-*image* actualising, they may *hide* what they really think, feel or want in order to win approval:

Robert Houseman

Robert Houseman, a Senior Partner, described how he finds sales calls with colleagues far more stressful than when he's alone. When he's on his own he's completely absorbed by the client's issues and totally focused on the matter at hand. He's passionate about his own business, loves solving problems and intuitively leads conversations to a mutually satisfactory close. During one-to-one meetings, therefore, he comes over as charismatic, genuine and likeable. What gives him a kick out of such sales calls is both the response he gets from the client plus, of course, getting the order.

On the other hand, he dreads sales calls with his partners who attempt to undermine him in the eyes of his subordinates and the client. He performs badly because he is *unfocused*. He not only feels responsible for getting the order but is also concerned to be seen as the best. During these meetings, because his mind flits in and out of the subject of the conversation, even for a matter of seconds, to focus on *how* he is performing (ego management) rather than simply on *doing it*, he is ineffective. As a result he feels angry with himself for turning off the client and losing the order and with his partners for sabotaging his efforts. Each negative experience produces more anxiety before the next meeting and so a downward spiral of failure ensues.

An individual's passion for excellence can be doused by their preoccupation with their performance. No matter what the climate, this *preoccupation affects concentration* on the task at hand. Perls *et al.* (1951, p. 29) have defined two types of concentration:

---

1   *Spontaneous concentration*, which is something that is *difficult to stop ourselves doing*. We pay attention where our interests lie and become totally absorbed and we come across as authentic, for example, when we are working at the computer for what seems like 10 minutes and find it's been over an hour.

2   *Deliberate concentration*, which is something that we have to *make ourselves do*. We 'pay' attention where we 'ought to' in order to self-image actualise by summoning up our energy and compelling ourselves whilst at the same time attempting to withhold attention from our real needs or interests.

When individuals are focused on the *impression* they're making and fall into deliberate concentration, they become inward-looking, anxious, preoccupied and perform badly. The anxiety is concerned with the role they're playing and they use negative self-talk to wind themselves up: 'Will my role as Senior Partner come off?' 'Will I be called a good girl?' 'Will they think I'm the best?' 'Will the audience applaud warmly or will they think I'm stupid and inept?' 'Will I get asked back next year?' This results in a downward spiral of ineffective behaviour, negative feedback and introspection, as shown in Figure 20.

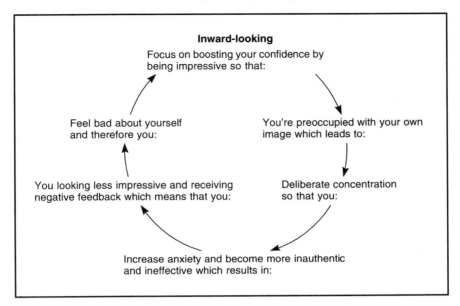

Figure 20   The downward spiral of trying to impress

A switch between spontaneous and deliberate concentration – and hence *effectiveness* – can occur, for example, whilst giving a presentation. At the outset of the presentation, the speaker is absorbed, enthused and fluent. He is spontaneously concentrating. Suddenly, he notices that certain members of the audience, for their own ego management reasons, are clearly hostile to his ideas. He becomes anxious and preoccupied with their vibes, loses confidence and fluency and fumbles over the next three slides. He is deliberately concentrating and bluffs his way through, knowing his argument has lost direction and has become lightweight, unconvincing and inauthentic. Someone genuinely interested asks a question with which he's fully conversant and he's focused again and back to spontaneous concentration.

At the end of presentation when he's comfortable he can take any question from anyone no matter how personal or difficult. Indeed it's quite enjoyable dealing skilfully with a saboteur amongst the group. When, on the other hand, he's still preoccupied with the quality of his performance, even the most innocuous question can throw him.

Don't impress – *be* impressed

One way to avoid preoccupation with our impression is to remember that we are not unique in our fears. Everyone is worrying about the impression they make on others. But because of their high profile, it's probably most noticeable when CEOs, MDs, and Managers behave this way. Some executives try to play the role of competent, knowledgeable, infallible leader. To hide their true vulnerability they become aloof, aggressive or absent. But no one is fooled. Fritz Perls (1971) makes this point in his distinction between the adult and the mature person:

> ‘An adult is in my opinion a person who plays a role of an adult, and the more he plays the role, the more immature he often is (to another person).’ (*p. 29*)

When senior management keep their distance or make others keep their distance or hold their tongues or make others hold their tongues, it rarely impresses. Avoiding the opinions of others doesn't change them, and it usually makes them worse.

Brian Redford

Brian Redford, an MD, was encouraged during a culture-change programme to be open and listen to the negative points being made, acknowledge them and deal with them. His inclination was to close these conversations down because he thought as an MD he was above criticism. The point is if you don't hear the criticism it won't go away. It just gets worse. No one is fooled by the role being played.

If individuals attempt to genuinely listen and see themselves, the organisation, relationships and so on through the eyes of others they begin a dialogue that might finally solve the problem, make the relationship closer, increase motivation and productivity.

When Brian let down his defences and really listened authentically, non-judgementally and empathically he began to impress his staff and win them over. When he listened empathically and *did* something about it, he could lead them anywhere! *Then* the employees were truly impressed.

It's much easier to relax and be authentic if individuals stop focusing on maintaining their own *self-worth* and instead focusing on enhancing the *self-esteem of others*:

> Don't try and impress others. Be impressed by them. Then you'll really be impressive.

Focusing on building the confidence of others begins an upward spiral of mutual honesty, trust and authenticity, as illustrated in Figure 21.

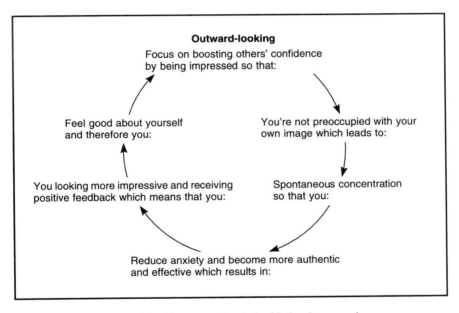

Figure 21   The upward spiral of being impressed

In sum

To go back to Robert Houseman, the Senior Partner, when he tried to be impressed he became so focused on boosting the egos of his colleagues that he no longer thought about himself and so the upward spiral began. He found he could win business equally well on his own as with colleagues.

The more individuals focus on building others' self-esteem and making them feel OK the less deliberate their concentration and the more OK they feel about themselves. Paradoxically, when individuals have no thought of the impression they are making they give a brilliant performance and make a great impression. When individuals focus on their personal agenda and self-image actualise, they lose the freedom to self-actualise for the benefit of themselves and the organisation.

13 The Conflict is Within, not Without

> *The inner enemy is as much a formidable foe as the most manipulative associate.*
>
> (*George Bach*)

Being passionate

The ideal organisation is one where each and every employee has a passion for excellence but some people have *never felt passionate* about anything.

I was walking into a video shop the other day when I heard a father say to his son aged about four, 'I want doesn't get!' With this, the little boy's excitement instantly evaporated as he controlled his emotions and walked in poker faced. If the only way to get what you want is to control your natural enthusiasm and pretend indifference, and you do this for long enough, it is no wonder that later on in life, it is difficult to dredge up any enthusiasm and passion for anything. As Clive James puts it in his novel *The Silver Castle* (1996):

> *He was still a child in that way, not thinking of the wished-for thing in case whatever forces that might grant it would deny it.*

Some people learnt a long time ago that they do not have the *right* to wish, want or feel, were made to feel guilty, bad or stupid if they did and so in an attempt to avoid these feelings they learnt to *suppress* wanting, wishing, hoping, having and so on.

Likewise, if parents make promises they never keep and constantly let their children down, they lower and lower their sights until they will not allow themselves to hope for anything from anyone. They don't trust words. What's worse, because they are powerless to control their own destiny, they eventually expect nothing from themselves. They don't trust *themselves*. So now *their* words and promises have no meaning. To avoid disappointment they not only deaden themselves to their wants, wishes and feelings but also make no effort to achieve since they are bound to fail. It was easier to fall in with the culture of the family and accept that very little gets achieved than to be passionate, hopeful and constantly disappointed. Their behaviour in the organisation is merely a continuation of dealing with disappointment. They exemplify 'rocking horse management' – lots of activity but never getting anywhere.

Rather than surface feelings, wants, desires and passions in the present and acting with a sense of purpose, some people instead live in the past, some in the future and some become cold and robotic.

Daydreaming about the past

Those who avoid feelings by daydreaming about the past do so in order to find excuses for their *present* predicament. Although adult behaviour is based on childhood experiences it does not help solve present problems to blame the past.

When individuals remember the past as *negative* and focus on how others treated them – their parents, colleagues, managers, teachers – these memories are important in the present only if they help them see that they are repeating patterns in their present situation. Otherwise the focus on the past is just a pretence at solving their current problems whilst in reality it is simply a convenient way of avoiding them.

By looking to the past, blaming others, they remain forever a child. They are not taking responsibility for the choices *they* are currently free to make. They abdicate responsibility for the situation they find themselves in and in so doing they relinquish their own personal power and control over their life by giving themselves an *excuse not to act*.

Alternatively, if instead individuals remember the past as exceptionally *positive* as 'the perfect childhood' or the 'best years of their life' they're once again using the past to escape their responsibility to make the decisions that would alleviate their present frustrations. Equally, by glamourising their past, they may be neglecting the many positive aspects of their life in the present which they could use as a foundation to build a 'glamorous' future.

Daydreaming about the future

At the opposite extremes are the individuals who only live for the *future*. They plan and dream either about how they fear it will be or about how they hope it will be. They try to be, however impossible, always one step ahead of what actually is.

If individuals fear the future because they lack belief that they can deal with life, they view it as *negative*. They rehearse for every event and then have no ability to act spontaneously when it arrives whilst situations for which they have failed to prepare catch them utterly at a loss. Either that or they take the most convoluted route and complicate every issue. Nothing is simple, no solution is the obvious one. They always see the worst. *They don't act.*

Recently I was working with two clients who were starting a new business that seemed to be a great opportunity. The one partner had made the decision and was seeking advice on the best method to proceed. The other was in effect still considering it. Her focus was on preparing analyses and was thereby avoiding making the decision. If these two approaches are not used to support each other then there is the potential for company politics. Their attitudes would polarise, the decisive partner would become even more decisive and cavalier in his approach and the indecisive partner would become ever more cautious. Consensus decisions would become impossible and the bad feelings created by this rift would seep out in sabotage, each seeking support for their position with staff or customers.

If, on the other hand, their view of the future is *positive* individuals are dealing with their present problems by avoiding them with daydreams, resolutions and promises. Their hope for tomorrow is a means of putting off doing something today.

Some salesmen, rather than ask the really tough questions to qualify a sale will spend energy and effort pursuing the opportunity and make a 'genuine' revenue forecast built on a fantasy. Since they have never asked pertinent questions, as far as they are concerned it is a real opportunity. They filter out any negatives and accentuate the positives. By so doing, they avoid feeling the anxiety of either losing the sale or implementing it by not working with people who are serious buyers. In effect, they cannot lose this order. They never have to make a promise or make it work and because there is no decision to be made no decision is ever made. It is always an opportunity for the future.

Then there are those who use the excuse of *uncertainty* about the future to avoid involving themselves in what is certain – namely the present. If the future is uncertain what's the point of putting an effort into anything today? They could be wasting their time, so why bother? They avoid disappointment by minimising the expectations of themselves and others. Not wanting anything or feeling anything means that they can never be disappointed or hurt.

With both types of individual, the company politics arise because others who do not understand that they live in a daydream world base their activities on the promises and decisions made, not realising that they have no intentions of carrying them out. Their unreliability creates resentment, anger and low morale and is the basis of inertia both within and between departments.

Rather than confront the present reality they either excuse their performance or blame somebody else for their failure. Rarely if ever is their propensity to live in a dream world confronted. Because they're not dealing with realities, making a 'decision' has no relation to acting upon it. In effect, they haven't made a decision.

Being cold and robotic

Still others become cold and robotic. When individuals cannot feel, want or wish for themselves, they model themselves on the standards of their reference group or on rational argument. To the observer they may seem mechanical, predictable and lifeless:

> 'To make a point of maximising automatic functioning . . . is the goal of the cybernetics worker in reverse – instead of trying, as they do, to make robots which are more and more like men, it is an attempt to make oneself more and more a robot.'
>
> (*Perls et al., 1951*)

Their behaviour is highly inflexible and predictable. In an effort to avoid feeling vulnerable, rejected or disappointed, they decide that it's better not to want, feel or wish. Instead, they *appear strong by acting tough.*

They are control-mad, but end up being controlled, for example, by forcing themselves to stick to the most inconvenient plan or trying to impose controls on those around them who continue to do what they want secretly or hide their mistakes. Instead of being in control they are controlled by their own rules or by the secrecy of others.

They do not feel empty or directionless. No rocking-horse management here. On the contrary, they are active, forceful, possessed with a sense of urgency and purpose at all times and achieve. But there are times when they have a glimpse of doubt and realise that though they have a purpose, it is not their purpose; and though they have desires and goals, they are not their own. They are so busy, so driven that they feel they have neither the time nor the right to ask themselves who they really are, what they really want. They end up either with a chip on their shoulder or constantly looking over their shoulder. Under these circumstances it's difficult, if not impossible, to be passionate about anything.

When desires, wishes, ideals and deep-seated personal values are based on external rules and authority, it's no surprise that while they can be passionate about rule-following autocracy, they lack a sense of urgency or focus when asked to be passionate about flexible autonomy and self-actualisation.

Unconscious feelings and desires block our actions

Organisations attempt to motivate individuals by intellectualisation, discussion, shouting, rationalisation, rewarding, threatening or pleading for change. Yet when individuals don't do what they say they will do, it should not be assumed that it is in their power to 'snap out of it,' since the feelings, fears, wishes and wants which influence their will to change are often *unconscious*. Change for some cannot be made by deliberate decision, except very superficially. To change, individuals have to bring the resisters to awareness and deal with them themselves. So wanting something has no causal relationship to acting:

---

* What a man does when he wants, is no evidence for his wanting. *
                                          (Melden, 1961, p. 166)

Individuals say they want to diet, mean it and yet continue to eat junk food; say they want to support the new culture, mean it, but continue to be negative and uncooperative; say they want to change, mean it, but don't. When individuals don't do what they *say* they want to do they are often as perplexed as those around them. Even as they eat the chocolate or moan about the culture they are totally baffled at their own lack of resolve.

Wanting can influence behaviour but it cannot replace *will*. When individuals decide but do not act we say they have 'no will power'. According to Farber (1966) individuals can't *deliberately* will themselves to change because there are *two realms of the will*, and whilst one is conscious and can be influenced, the other is unconscious and cannot therefore be tapped directly:

> ‘I can will knowledge, but not wisdom; going to bed, but not sleeping; eating, but not hunger; meekness, but not humility; scrupulosity, but not virtue; self-assertion or bravado, but not courage; lust, but not love; commiseration, but not sympathy; congratulations, but not admiration; religiosity, but not faith; reading, but not understanding.’ *(p. 15)*

Individuals want to be courageous but unconsciously they want recognition from authority. Insomniacs want to sleep but unconsciously their feelings of guilt, fear or anxiety won't let them. Individuals decide to lose weight and reduce intake of food but unconsciously they want comfort. It's known that certain eating disorders are more about a cry for power and control over the life of the individual than about trying to look slim.

If culture change programmes, by definition, are looking for personal change and action then such programmes must surely attempt to *influence the will*. As Rabbi Nachman put it:

> ‘There are no obstacles that one cannot overcome, for the obstacle is only there on account of the will and in truth there are no obstacles but psychic ones.’

Those who live with, work with or manage those who say one thing and constantly do another will know that overcoming the 'psychic' obstacles is no easy task. As Yalom (1980) puts it:

> ‘I sometimes think of the will . . . as a turbine encased and concealed by ponderous layers of metal. I know that the vital moving part is lodged deep in the innards of the machine. Puzzled, I circle it. I try to affect it from a distance, by exhortation, by poking tapping or incantation. by performing those rites that I have been led to believe will influence it. These rites require much patience and much blind faith . . . What is required is a more expedient rational approach to the will.’
>
> (*p. 292*)

When individuals blame others for their situation, in many cases it is they themselves who block their own action with *unconscious resisters*. Their conflict is *internal*.

The conflict is within us, not without

One of the most common internal conflicts is between *Topdog* and *Underdog* (Perls, 1971). The Topdog is authoritarian and thinks he knows best. As Perls puts it: 'He is sometimes right, but always righteous.' Topdog says things like: 'You should,' and 'You should not,' and manipulates with threats of catastrophe, such as: 'If you don't then – you'll be disliked, you'll look ridiculous, you'll go to hell, you'll be a failure,' and so on.

The Underdog is also manipulative but does so by being weak, helpless, submissive, whining and apologetic. The Underdog says things like: 'I do my best.' 'I'm as worried as you are,' 'I'm trying – *really*,' 'No one could do better,' 'I work as hard as anyone,' 'I can't help it if I forgot,' 'I'll change, I *mean* it, really.'

This is the inner conflict, the struggle between the Topdog and the Underdog to gain control. Because individuals are not conscious of their inner conflict they find themselves stuck between the part of them that wants to 'fly' and the part that 'nails their foot to the floor'. When individuals identify either with their Topdog or Underdog they don't realise their own part in blocking themselves and may disown (*project*) it onto mother, father, society, management, the company culture, lack of communication etc. They may even assist in their own impasse by choosing a partner who exhibits the opposing characteristic and play out the conflict between Topdog and Underdog forever.

Thus, individuals maintain the status quo and continue their life of a mediocre mentality, a mediocre existence, a mediocre career, a mediocre marriage because they can see no way through the impasse. If they can become aware of, identify with and own both sides of the internal conflict, they become more *balanced, centred*, and *act*.

Shifting our inner conflict to an open conflict

Action can result from shifting the 'inner conflict' between wishes and counter-attacking resistances into an *open, aware conflict*.

Claire Morrell

Claire Morrell is an executive who assumed that everyone around her was obstructing her work by being passive, lazy and negative. She blamed others for damaging her career, wasting her life and affecting her health. She dealt with these saboteurs either by deferring or losing her cool. Claire played out the following dialogue between her Topdog and Underdog:

Topdog:	You should be more assertive and more confrontational. You don't have to put up with this behaviour.
Underdog:	It's all very well for you but I have to live with these people every day. I don't want to be made to look the bad one.
Topdog:	That's typical of you, wimp – you always hold me back.
Underdog:	Yeah and you always stick me in it. Why can't you control yourself?
Topdog:	If I controlled myself we'd never get anything done.
Underdog:	And if I went banging around, we'd have no one cooperating with us at all.
Topdog:	OK, I see your point but that doesn't diminish my input.
Underdog:	Well I'll be less avoiding if you are less aggressive.
Topdog:	OK but I don't know how to start changing.
Underdog:	Neither do I, but I'm willing to make a start . . .

Conversations between two resisters can give individuals an insight into the way they *sabotage themselves*. As the two fragments continue the dialogue, the Topdog becomes calmer and the Underdog less defensive and they begin to seek and agree solutions. Individuals develop new ideas and a new perspective.

Can do/can't do

One of the most common splits in an individual's personality is between the part that believes they can do anything and the part that tells them they're not up to it. This is when individuals suffer from a crisis of confidence. *One part* of them says: 'I'm brilliant at what I do,' 'No one else is as good as I am,' 'I should be famous,' 'I could run the business better than he can.' The *other part* says: 'I'm hopeless,' 'What I do is pointless, I'm nothing,' 'Anyone can do what I do,' 'I've nothing special to say,' 'I'm stupid.'

Paula McGregor

Paula McGregor, an accountant and business development manager, frequently suffered panic attacks at work. She was keen to leave and set up in her own business since she felt she was undervalued in her current position. Yet no matter how many times she went over the pros and cons of each choice, she could not decide. During one session she decided to have her Topdog and Underdog converse with each other.

Paula discovered that her Topdog was telling her that she's special, accomplished, can achieve anything she wants, is far shrewder than her Managing Director, is stronger than others and has made all the right enquiries into the prospective business to ensure minimal risk.

Her Underdog, however, nags at the back of her mind, especially when she is tired and vulnerable, and tells her she is inferior, unlikeable, is sure to fail, will be overwhelmed by such an ambitious plan, to keep her thoughts to herself, that everyone is looking at her in meetings, in trains and so on and that she should stop making herself look foolish.

The perpetual conflict between her Topdog and Underdog were her real source of anxiety. She was attempting to fly whilst nailing her own foot to the floor. The battle between the two kept her from knowing what she wanted and achieving it and so she stays the same. Topdog exaggerates and puts up ideas that are so risky that Underdog puts the brakes on. Paula is caught in the middle, simply doing what everyone else wants for fear of Topdog being found wanting and Underdog being proved right. No wonder she was getting non-specific anxiety attacks.

Everyone has a Topdog and Underdog to some extent, and feels powerful at times and inadequate at others.

We are full of opposites

Often individuals will find, as they have their inner conversation, that the two opposites change character. Individuals are *full of opposites*. Comediennes are often depressives and actors frequently suffer from chronic shyness.

Jonathan Bogdanovitch

Jonathan Bogdanovitch decided that he wanted to have a dialogue with *'Practical'* and *'Emotional'*, the two parts of his personality that he felt were keeping him stuck in an irrational position in life. He is 23 years old with a classics degree, living at home, deeply depressed, confused and unable to hold down a job. Whilst continually on the verge of tears, he is forever saying that he stays at home because it's easy, and comfortable. How could he say he was comfortable when he was on Prozac in deep depression? By convincing himself that his life was made easy by obtaining food, having his washing done, his room cleaned and tidied and money, he ignored the fact that he was also deeply depressed. So he decided to work with his two opposing sides the Practical and the Emotional one.

As they conversed, Jonathan realised that there was another split. He called these *'Conventional'* and *'Drop Out'*. His conventional one (Topdog) kept saying: 'You should be getting on with something, getting married, finding a job, buying a house' and so on and the Drop Out said: 'But I don't want to, I don't want that commitment, I'm not ready to settle down.' He was surprised to find that though he had always imagined his father saying the Conventional words the reality was that his father rarely if ever did. He was projecting his own Topdog onto his father. So then the split became between his internal *'Parent'* and *'Child'* and so on.

An individual's resistances often come from within by launching counterattacks against our own efforts and best interests.

In sum

If individuals were told, God forbid, that they had 6 months to live, they would certainly be clearer about what they wanted, able to decide and act. Such a confrontation with death tends to clarify their values. If they chose to continue to work they would no doubt be nothing but authentic, changing and confronting everything in sight! It would be easy because they would have 'nothing left to lose' What do individuals think they have to lose if they choose to do what's in their hearts *now*?

Individuals refrain from confronting, changing and acting because they fear that they will lose respect, lose friendship, lose admiration, lose the possibility of promotion, lose their security and lose their jobs. They fear that they would not only 'lose face' but may even lose their livelihood. But others cannot be judging them *before* the action. They are judging themselves with negative self-talk. They, or rather their fantasies, are therefore their *own* resisters. A benefit which comes from developing the ability to see their opposite side is that instead of being a person who feels they are always *being judged*, they realise that *they themselves are the one who do the judging*.

Understanding and overcoming our own resisters gives us the insight that we block ourselves and that we are free to act in a world that is more indifferent to our actions than we originally believed. No one except yourself, your values, attitudes, beliefs, fears and so on, stops you confronting company politics.

_____ **Self-Analysis** _____

Transforming resisters into assisters

This experiment is designed to make you aware of conflicts in your own personality and to show how the *resister* can be reclaimed and transformed into a valuable *assister*. Most conflict is between one part of our personality and another.

1 Try and imagine you are sitting in front of yourself right now. You can see an image of yourself as if you are looking in a mirror. Look at your face, your expression, have a quick glance at what you're wearing to make sure you are going to speak as this person.

2 Let this image of yourself have a dialogue beginning each sentence with the words: 'You should,' 'You must,' 'You ought,' or 'You shouldn't,' 'You ought not,' 'You must not'. This is your Topdog.

3 Now be yourself and reply to these demands. Notice your tone of voice as you imagine yourself replying. This is your Underdog.

4 Next be the Topdog image of yourself; again reply to your Underdog.

5 Keep the conversation going until you come to some conclusion or insight.

14 So Your Indecision is Final?

Vladimir: Shall we go?
Estragon: Let's go.
[*Stage directions: No one moves.*]   (*Samuel Beckett*)

Shallow agreements and company politics

In Samuel Beckett's *Waiting for Godot* (1956) the characters reflect, plan, resolve and procrastinate but never act. The play ends with the following:

> Vladimir: Shall we go?
> Estragon: Let's go.
> [*Stage directions: No one moves.*]

This example of '*abortive decision-making*' (Yalom, 1980) sums up what's happening in many team meetings throughout organisations. Someone makes a suggestion, everyone 'agrees', an apparent decision is made but, in effect, 'no one moves'.

Jaap van Meeren

Jaap van Meeren, the European Sales Director of an IT company, contributed to the culture of game-playing and dishonesty by making agreements that he never kept. For example:

- He told the staff in a Belgian town that he would keep the office open, when subsequently they found him arranging to move the office to Brussels
- He told the British sales team he would be in Britain on certain days, and wouldn't turn up
- He told the Dutch employees that he'd sign all contracts, expenses and payroll cheques every Friday, but was frequently somewhere else on the day.

His excuse was always that something 'more important' had come up that had greater priority. In effect, when Jaap said he would do something he was adding silently and in parenthesis: 'I will do this unless something turns up that is personally more interesting and more important.'

The fact that he never committed to agreements indicates that he had *never really decided*. If no action follows a decision clearly there has been no true decision, merely '*a flirt* with decision' (Yalom, 1980) or a '*shallow agreement*' with others, but most importantly, with ourselves.

Because there was a mismatch between what he said and what he did, others accused Jaap of sabotaging them by his 'lack of commitment'. But it wasn't a problem of commitment, it was a problem of *indecision*. If individuals really want something, they decide to go for it and then they act on the decision. They may want to buy their first home, they decide to do it, call the estate agent and buy one. Had Jaap *really decided* to do what he said he would do, the commitment would *automatically* have been there. Eventually Jaap's behaviour gave everyone permission to sabotage everyone else with shallow agreements to which they were not committed. In effect, his inability to decide created the culture.

To know and not to act is not to know at all

'Shall we go. Let's go. No one moves.' The culture of many organisations, like Harlow Systems in Chapter 4, could be described by these 3 short sentences just 3 months into a change programme. When the programme is put in place, people have the hope that finally, this time, the company politics will be acknowledged and dealt with. The management think it will be dealt with by the 'programme', the consultants and staff and the employees think it will be dealt with by the management. Because initially they are hopeful, most individuals enthusiastically make promises to change both their own behaviour and their working practice, promises which at the time they really mean to keep.

Because there is a mismatch between the decision to change and the hope that somebody else will do it, when others *don't* change they are accused of sabotaging the programme by their 'lack of commitment'. But had any one of them really decided to 'move', the commitment would *automatically* have been there.

For individuals to make a decision means to commit themselves to a course of *action*. When individuals 'decide' night after night to confront people in their team, leave the company or speak frankly to their managers, it's not their inability to commit to the decision that prevents action, it is rather that they haven't really decided. Awareness of personal responsibility is not synonymous with change. They've only reached the threshold of change. They need to move beyond awareness to action. In the words of a Japanese proverb:

> To know and not to act is not to know at all.

Shallow agreements and lack of commitment stem from the fact that there has never been a true decision.

Why is it so difficult to make decisions?

Wheelis (1956) in the following metaphor describes both those who are unaware that decisions mean a commitment to action and therefore *never get to the cross-roads* and those who are *at the cross-roads but cannot decide*:

> 'Some persons can proceed untroubled by proceeding blindly, believing they have travelled the main highway and that all intersections have been with byways. But to proceed with awareness and imagination is to be affected by the memory of cross-roads which one will never encounter again. Some persons sit at the cross-road, taking neither path because they cannot take both, cherishing the illusion that if they sit there long enough the two ways will resolve themselves into one and hence both be possible.'

Both these blocks could apply to the same person simultaneously. For example, Jaap's Sales Manager in Amsterdam, Joslein Kruisselberge, not long after she joined the company, told him that his sales forecast was worthless because in her judgement none of the opportunities listed were properly 'qualified'. Jaap refused to make the decision to adjust the figures. Rather he went away thinking to himself that even if the forecast is halved it's OK. It was easier to keep on fooling himself and hope the figures would come right, than decide to change the figures or change the sales strategy and be accountable for acting on the decision.

Such people frequently lack confidence and therefore have well activated ego-defence mechanisms such as denial and avoidance. They believe their own propaganda and don't realise they are not deciding. Because of his pretence Jaap 'proceeded blindly' down the 'highway', all 'byways' being the different routes he *could* have taken were he to deal with the present and decide

In Jaap's case the underlying cause of proceeding blindly was the result of sitting at a cross-road in the attempt to make a bigger decision that he wouldn't make. He constantly debated in his mind whether to leave the Company or retrieve his sole control of Benelux. His superficial behaviour at work was covering his deep discontent and inability to decide. Many individuals are struggling with major decisions in their lives and the consequences of this indecision is indifference to less meaningful ones. Until their life decision is resolved all other decisions seem comparatively trivial and so they ask themselves 'Why bother?'

Sitting at the cross-roads 'taking neither path because they cannot take both' is something most people can identify with at some point in their lives. For example, when they consider a change in lifestyle, leaving one relationship for another or moving from employment to self-employment. They can neither decide to say 'Yes' nor to say 'No'. They endlessly weigh up the pros and cons, decide which way they want to jump, yet remain hovering in limbo.

Straining forward with the foot on the brake

Yet those who are at the cross-roads in fact suffer far more discomfort than hovering in limbo, as described by Fritz Perls *et al.* (1951) in their metaphor:

> ⁶The pilot of a carrier-based plane must take off from a short runway. Unless he can attain speed sufficient to support him in the air by the time he reaches the end of the deck, he will simply drop off into the water. To minimise this hazard he first 'revs up' his engine, while his brakes, fully applied, hold him stationary. Then, when his motor is whirling the propeller at such a rate that the plane shakes, throbs, strains at the brakes, he suddenly releases them and flashes into the air. Until this point the pilot, identifying himself with his ship, might verbalise his sense of the opposed forces by saying: '*I feel the tremendous urge to fly, but also the equal and opposite tendency to hold back. If I kept this up for long, it would shake me to pieces.*' And, of course, the whole manoeuvre would be completely senseless if there were not the clear intention, when the right moment came, to release the brake and take off.⁹ (*p. 72*)

They are not merely hovering in limbo but are, in fact, *tearing themselves apart*. When caught in indecision they experience it more as *straining forward with the foot on the brake* which is one of extreme conflict – the conflict between moving and not moving rather than idling in neutral, or hovering in limbo. They are neither unaware of a decision nor idling but continually wrestling with the internal struggle of an agonising decision, a moral choice.

Rebecca Gardner

Rebecca Gardner, a research chemist, wants to work in Canada but is afraid of failure. This urge to go to Canada is blocking her from focusing on her career in the UK. So she is failing. She's constantly straining forward because every fibre of her body wants to leave for her new life yet she holds herself back with her foot on the brake. Rebecca has *decided to tear herself apart.*

Alternatives exclude

Why do people struggle and sit at the cross-roads? One reason is that to decide one thing means having to *give up something else*.

Sanjay Patel

Sanjay Patel, a Civil Servant, was finding it hard to commit to any decisions made at work. He was at a cross-roads in his personal life as he had the choice between succumbing to his parents' wishes by putting his wife second or leaving the family home. The hardest thing in our lives is to let go of our options knowing they may never come again. The existential implication of choice is that 'alternatives exclude' (Gardner, 1971, p. 115): for every 'yes' there must be a 'no.' Decisions are painful because they remind us that, like everyone else, our life consists of a limited number of possibilities. We attempt to avoid awareness of the limitation of possibilities by avoiding making a decision.

In Søren Kierkegaard's book *Either/Or* (cited in D. Lodge, *Therapy*, 1996, p. 108), one of his characters believes that either/or, it doesn't matter what you choose, you will always regret your choice. 'If you marry, you will regret it, if you do not marry, you will regret it; if you marry or do not marry, you will regret both'. We ask ourselves: What will happen if we cross the Rubicon and we've made a mistake? And so we vacillate. As the hero of David Lodge's novel *Therapy* (1996, p. 111) puts it: 'My indecision is final, as the man said'.

Sanjay chose his wife and lost his close relationship with his parents along with their approval. Sanjay defined the moment and by so doing he defined himself.

The delusion of specialness

The limitations of possibilities also threaten an individual's 'delusion of specialness'. They feel that though others may be restricted, they are special in that they can have it all, if they just hold on.

Sanjay could not have both his wife's love and his parents' love. He chose to define the moment and now regrets the loss of his parents and the loss of his belief that he is special and can have it all. He could, however, have sat at the cross-roads hoping that both would merge into one in which case the moment would have defined him. He would have lost himself. Although we may regret our decision we need to remember that we regret our indecision too!

Geoffrey Adler

Geoffrey Adler, the MD of a European Division of a major German corporation, couldn't decide whether to put up with the never-ending company politics in his team and company or to take the chance of starting his own business. He had been vacillating for 12 months. This major life decision meant that company decisions were downgraded in his mind. For example, he made a top team decision about the company structure which had major implications for everyone's future but which he had no intention of seeing through. This blatant lack of interest was obvious to everyone, although not the reason for it. Finally he was sacked and became so demoralised that he didn't have the confidence to start the new business either.

People wait because they are frightened they'll get it wrong and then they regret their indecision. So paradoxically, in hoping to have it all, rather than take a new path and decide, they stand still and stay on the same road with the same scenery. One reason for shallow agreements in organisations is that individuals are struggling with a major life decision which, in contrast, trivialises all other aspects of their existence. They should not forget that decisions may signify the limitation of possibilities but they are the only way to open up new and more possibilities.

Seeing yourself from a different perspective

> I know a couple who have grown apart to the point that John wishes to leave. Judy has always threatened to leave, to file for divorce and generally expressed her unhappiness within the marriage. Recently, John said: 'I've had enough too, I want a divorce'. Even though Judy was absolutely convinced that for the past 20 years she had been saying what she really meant, she had, in fact, never really decided because 'to decide and not to act is not to decide at all'. Therefore John by saying what he did, made the decision for her. By saying I'm going, *he* made the decision. By supporting Judy's decision John has acted on Judy's behalf by moving out and initiating the split.
>
> Now Judy has to deal with the reality rather than the fantasy. The reality is that she is now on her own, with limited job skills and earning capacity, tied to the responsibility of children and feels that she can't cope alone. These are the realities that, by not really deciding, she has unconsciously avoided thinking about.

Making a decision can shift individuals from their everyday experience to an *ontological* one where they see themselves objectively as a Being who is totally alone in the world. For some this shift in perspective can be a liberating experience whilst for others it's a very threatening experience which they avoid by avoiding decisions.

David Selnick

David Selnick, the MD of a software consultancy company, couldn't decide whether he wanted to work towards becoming the Chairman of the company or to go and do Voluntary Service Overseas (VSO). He had battled through the politics and game-playing of the company for 30 years and was tired of it. He had been going over and over the decision in his mind for at least 4 years and still couldn't decide. He didn't need the money, neither did his family and so this was not part of the decision-making process. The real problem was that every time he thought of doing VSO work it confronted him with a clear perspective on his life and values and his choice between continuing to strive and achieve in the eyes of others or to do what he wanted and possibly be negatively judged. Each time he 'decided' it forced him to see himself as being on his own.

When individuals are suddenly confronted with this fact, fear may overwhelm them and they begin to question what it is they really want. They see the *possibility of recreating themselves but fear letting go* of all the accoutrements that provide them with their self-concept.

The only way to avoid wasting their life sitting at the cross-road is either to view their current situation positively or take the risk and view the ambiguity as an inevitable consequence of a new and richer life.

You're on your own

No one can decide for David Selnick, or make it easier. He alone has to decide, he alone has to act and he alone has to live with the consequences of his decision. A decision is, therefore, a lonely act. It is each individual's *own* act and no one can decide for them. Decision therefore threatens their belief in the existence of an *ultimate rescuer* – someone who by condoning the decision can reassure the person, give them strength, share the blame and protect them from criticism; someone who will give them permission, give them their blessing and make it safe. Since there are no ultimate rescuers their decisions will always confront them with the fact that *existentially they are on their own.*

Some avoid decisions by letting others make them for them but then find their lives wasted. David Selnick's current dilemma stems from his interview with IBM 30 years previously when, as a graduate trainee, much to his surprise, they decided he was not an analyst programmer, which was the job he went for, but a salesman. In fact, David has many good qualities but he could not close business. So for the next 30 years he has been doing a job for which he was not suited and because he was failing he *played politics to shift responsibility* for the blame: the product doesn't work, the staff are wrong, the market is wrong and so on.

Had he realised at the initial interview that there are no ultimate rescuers, he may not have believed that this person knew something that he did not. He would therefore have rejected the advice and instead responded to his own feelings, which were telling him that he was no salesman.

Existentialist literature such as Jean-Paul Sartre's *Nausea* (1965), Albert Camus' *The Stranger* (1946) and Franz Kafka's *Metamorphosis* (1992) is full of lonely heroes. In the existential view, the fact that ultimately individuals are on their own is *not* something that can be remedied but something that must be *accepted and incorporated into their actions*. Human beings are alone. No one else can make their choices for them, nor can anyone else absorb the risks that those choices entail.

Existential guilt

As a result of David Selnick's belief in an ultimate rescuer he had a second issue to deal with. 30 years on he has a well-paid job and status yet he sits and wonders why he is doing it and suffering the guilt and remorse of a wasted life as a consequence. Part of his inability to make the decision to leave the company or to stop playing politics is this *existential guilt*.

If individuals make a decision to change, they are confronted with the fact that if they can change now they could equally have changed long ago. If they accept that they are responsible for their life now, then they must accept that they have always been responsible for it. By refusing to choose to change they attempt to avoid accepting their existential guilt for the damage they have done to themselves by living a wasted life of untapped possibilities.

Tony Smith

Tony Smith, a food technologist, was a devious and manipulative character who superficially was charming and helpful. Because of his constant game-playing behind the back of the MD, others in the organisation knew not to mess with him. One of his favourite games was to suck people into thinking he was on their side and then turn on them. For example, during a meeting regarding a product launch, he constantly supported Susan Gray the Marketing Director's views against the others bolstering her confidence. He then introduced some statistics which clearly indicated to the MD that her figures for the potential market were unrealistic. Susan, having been sucked into trusting him and then shown up by him, vowed to take revenge.

Tony rationalised his own behaviour on the grounds that everyone is the same, it's a dog-eat-dog world. When it was put to him that there were alternative ways of behaving, more honest and helpful, he was confronted with the knowledge that he had behaved obnoxiously throughout his life by convincing himself that everyone was the same so he had no choice. To decide to change his behaviour now would confront him with the knowledge that he could have changed 20 years ago and with the existential guilt of a wasted life.

Yet individuals cannot undo or atone for the past other than by deciding to change in the present, and so change their future. To avoid the present in order to avoid the guilt will merely perpetuate the situation.

I am able but unwilling

Rather than cross the Rubicon individuals sit at the crossroads. There are many ways that they stop themselves deciding. In a culture of shallow agreements and no commitment they excuse the fact that they cannot decide by saying:

> - I can't take any more
> - I don't know what I want
> - I can't decide
> - I can't go on
> - I have no idea what's going on
> - I have no idea how I feel.

Yet existentially *every act is preceded by a decision*. Individuals:

> - Decide they can't take any more
> - Decide they don't know what they want
> - Decide they can't decide
> - Decide they can't go on
> - Decide they have no idea what's going on
> - Decide they have no idea how they feel.

This is how individuals *depower* themselves and make excuses for the fact that 'No one moves'. Yet they are really metaphors (Taubman, 1994, pp. 110–11) that represent their current experience. By expressing the same situation differently, they can be honest with themselves, in touch with their real feelings and feel in a powerful position from which to decide to act. Look at Table 8.

Table 8 Deciding to act

Depowering excuse	*Current experience*
I can't take any more	I *can* continue to work in a negative environment but I wish certain individuals would stop sabotaging my efforts; this job is extremely stressful
I don't know what I want	I *know* what I want: I want a number of different things, but I'm not willing to choose one of them
I can't decide	I'm not willing to make a decision because any decision I make will have a *downside* to it and I'm just not willing to accept that right now
I can't go on	I can and will go on but quite honestly I've had enough and I want out; I wish I could either run away, be seriously ill or die so that the problem is *solved for me*
I have no idea what's going on	I know exactly what's going on around me, but the idea of doing something about the situation is so *threatening* I'd prefer not to think about it or get involved
I have no idea how I feel.	I am aware of my feelings, but it is far too *risky* to acknowledge any of them even to myself.

In sum

Decisions have different degrees of consciousness, effort, rationality, risk, courage, impulsiveness and sense of responsibility. Shallow agreements arise when individuals have not made a conscious decision, either because they are struggling with a major life decision or because their ego management issues are overriding their rationality and sense of responsibility.

Company politics arises out of such shallow agreements which affect almost every project undertaken. If organisations are to change, individuals must start to make fundamental personal changes and take responsibility for what they say and do rather than simply point the finger. Bringing each individual's decision-making process to a *conscious level* is one of the major contributions that can be made to prevent company politics.

15 How do I do it?

'If you meet the Buddha on the road, kill him!'

(Sheldon Kopp)

Inverting the iceberg

The core message of this book is that the responsibility for change, whether he likes it or not, rests with each and every individual to take action to confront the company politics that detract from the productivity of the organisation. Whilst much has been said in the past decade about instilling a 'Passion for Excellence' in organisations by creating a culture of shared values and goals in a safe climate little has been said to *mobilise passion and action on a personal level.* This is one of the main reasons why conventional culture change programmes have been so ineffective in the long term.

The fact is that certain individuals can be passionate about their work, be in a safe climate and still not behave passionately. A safe climate, as has been said before, is not enough. Neither is it necessary nor likely. Individuals who already possess the desired values cannot wait out their lives in the hope that others will create a climate where they feel so safe that they are prepared to risk being themselves. If they wait for safety, where's the risk? The risk of acting out the shared values only exists when they *act honestly in a hostile and distrusting environment.*

Learning to act in a hostile environment will not come about merely by developing individuals at Levels 1 and 2 of the iceberg model as has been the case in conventional culture change programmes (see Chapter 2). Rather, we need to *invert the iceberg,* as shown in Figure 22, in order for individuals to understand, learn and adopt the existential approach to being passionate about action.

- The task becomes to encourage individuals to discover that alternative possibilities exist where none were recognised before and that they themselves are able to make changes.
- To encourage than to explore the consequences of what they are doing right now, to weigh up the alternatives and make choices.

158

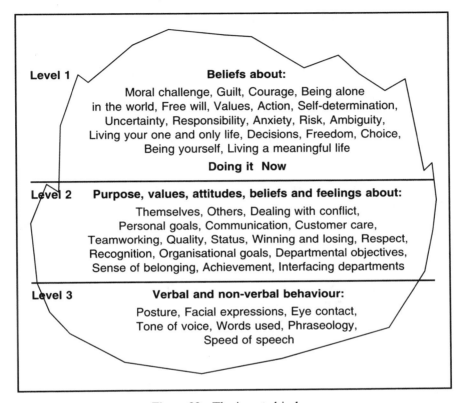

Figure 22   The inverted iceberg

- To recognise that whether they act or don't act will affect their personal situation and that they can hold no one else responsible for their existential decision. Some of the pragmatic fears that hold them back may be real, most are imaginary but in any case, the ultimate choice is between living a principled authentic life in pursuit of organisational goals or a personally unfulfilled one.

Existential education helps individuals recognise not only their personal responsibility for their actions but also to accept the inevitable *existential anxiety* that accompanies actions designed to change their situations. Many fear the weight of being responsible for who they are now and what they are becoming. They must choose whether to cling to the known and familiar fears or to risk opening themselves to a less certain and more challenging life. The lack of guarantees is what generates anxieties. Until individuals accept these Level 3 issues they will not confront company politics by taking the risk of using Level 2 and Level 1 skills, knowledge and techniques to change the organisation's culture.

Existentialists help individuals understand that they are responsible for *creating their own dispositions* – be they untrusting, game-playing, counterdependent, rule-following, inflexible, dependent, collaborative, focused or interdependent. Once everyone is aware that they are the author of their own dispositions they then become aware of their possibility of being disposed differently. There can be no blaming others.

Then and only then can the organisation introduce those dispositions valued by the management team at Level 2 of the iceberg. Only when individuals are aware of their responsibility for their past and of the stifling attitudes of their present, can they begin to accept responsibility for choosing their behaviour in the future.

To be disposed to collaborate, one must first choose collaboration. To be disposed to be honest, one must first choose honesty. To be disposed to sticking up for your principles one must first choose to do so. An education which reminds individuals that they are constantly, freely, creatively choosing in this way is the kind of education we are looking for. It is an education of private awareness and personal involvement.

The escalation of company politics

The examples of company politics in Case Study 15.1 are themselves trivial, but because individuals don't act to confront them, they escalate into the company culture which in turn effects productivity and profitability.

Bob Heyes

Bob Heyes is a very successful salesman but extremely aggressive and loud in conversations with staff and on the phone. He often uses abuse and swears obscenely. This makes it very difficult for those at neighbouring desks to concentrate on their work and is embarrassing if conducting a telephone conversation since clients can hear his noise in the background. He is very quick witted and therefore nobody takes the risk of confronting him for fear of being made to look stupid. The result is that those sitting near are less effective and the customer is turned off, may seek alternative sources of supply and the company's revenue and profits decline.

Stephanie Morris

Stephanie Morris is PA to the MD and also Office Manager. She habitually arranges the schedule for the 45-strong sales force to conduct their quarterly territory reviews with the MD which typically involves a presentation using between 10 and 12 slides. When one of the salesmen asked for some slides, she told him there were none left. When he asked why not she blamed the salesmen for the fact that they had not ordered them even though it was clearly her responsibility. He walked away and did not confront her. A repetition of such incidents will eventually lead to the salesman being overwhelmed by a feeling of pointlessness which he will carry into meetings, conversations and the customer site.

Ivan Selby

Ivan Selby, the Product Services Manager, is a chain smoker. It was agreed at a company meeting that there would be a no-smoking policy in the company. A smoking room was set aside on each floor for those who wished to smoke. Despite this, Ivan continued to smoke in his office. No one was prepared to confront him. The rest of the organisation felt resentful and revengeful and used his behaviour as permission to break other agreements and policies.

In each example, despite everyone obsessively talking about the behaviour of the individual concerned, no one will confront them. Instead, each incident led to wasted time and effort in corridor meetings and revenge cycles which in turn lead to, etc., etc. Whilst most individuals may feel a passion for doing their job and doing it professionally they do not confront the company politics that sabotage them.

It's like being in the middle of a battleground

We've seen that individuals don't confront for a number of reasons:

- Fear of being made to look stupid
- Apathy
- Too busy
- Not my problem
- Don't want to suffer retaliation
- Don't want to be disliked

- Disbelief that I can change anything
- Reluctance to create a pressure group because of the
- Suspicion that when you charge you'd be charging alone, with everyone else staying in the trenches.

The war analogy is interesting because many times during a days work, it can feel as if you're in the middle of a battlefield. People describe such an organisation culture as suffering from *inertia*. The definition of inertia is a 'body at rest unless disturbed by an external force', and since most people have no formal force with which to disturb things they feel as if they are left dealing with a body at rest with no personal power or control over their situation.

You're on your own

So individuals live with the hope that someone else will do it for them: the MD, the management, a braver colleague, a cleverer colleague, a stupider colleague, a member of their staff, the Chairman, the CEO and so on. Everyone points the finger, blames the other and sits in hope. Alternatively they hope for a head-hunter, a job opportunity or a partner to support them financially.

Yet if individuals sit and wait in the hope of someone else giving them permission, making things right or giving them the answer they'll wait forever. There are no answers, no right and wrong, no higher authorities. As Sheldon Kopp (1972) quoting the Zen masters, puts it:

> 'If you meet the Buddha on the road, kill him.' This admonition points up that no meaning that comes from outside ourselves is real. The only meaning in our lives is what we each bring to them. Killing the Buddha on the road means destroying the hope that anything outside of ourselves can be our master. No one is any bigger than anyone else, there are no mothers or fathers for grown-ups, only sisters and brothers. (*p. 140*)

In the end, each individual is on his or her own. The truth is there is no truth, we are all dealing with opinion.

I was making this point to a CEO of a large corporation recently when he jumped in to say that he couldn't have people doing their own thing. He argued that since he *is* right they have to do what he says. I put it to him that unless people either openly disagree with him and then agree to disagree and in the spirit of consensus do it his way or they leave the corporation, they will take the third option and sabotage. There is only opinion and they must be free to express theirs in response to his. It is in this sense that there is no right or wrong. Not only that, but even if he refuses to create the climate where they feel safe enough to do so, for the sake of their health and the company they must still take the risk and speak their mind. Until he and they realise that, he is left with option three: to live with sabotage or to sack them. Either way, he won't win.

Existentialism doesn't mean anarchy. What it does mean is that each individual has a personal obligation to express his views, however controversial. It means that all he can be sure of is the ambiguity and anxiety that accompanies his awareness of total responsibility for one human life – his own. All he can do is act, evaluate and act again. *There is no right answer.*

Many individuals cannot stand living a life which is such an *open-ended question.* Rather than accept this they pretend certainty and by so doing remain trapped in a web of their own self-deceit. They focus on the 'certain inevitability' of:

- feeding the family
- paying the mortgage
- being sacked for disagreeing
- needing to look good in the eyes of others
- disagreeable colleagues
- all companies are the same anyway
- not being able to do any better elsewhere
- having to be liked.

They constantly avoid dealing with the existential reality that, in the last analysis, they *define themselves with their own choices.* By making decisions they create their own suffering, misery frustration or discomfort.

Cross the Rubicon, or stay the same

So because of their hope that someone will save them along with the self-deception that they have no choice they actually make the choice to stand still in life rather than cross the Rubicon (Figure 23). They continue to suffer the existential guilt and stress of their current situation rather than the existential anxiety of crossing a Rubicon, trying something new and knowing that they're living their one and only life to the full. Despite their repeated experience that no one will save them they live with the 'triumph of hope over experience'.

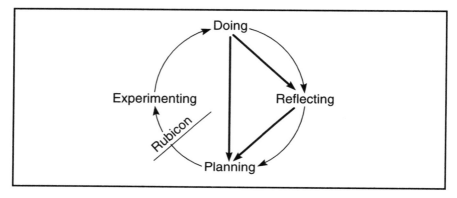

Figure 23   Cross the Rubicon, or stay the same

Whether they are contemplating dealing with an isolated incident of company politics, expressing their general discontent with sabotage to the management team or leaving the organisation for another post, they can't sit at the cross-roads forever. They can't sit and weigh up the pros and cons of the decision to stay or move hoping that both roads will merge into one or that someone will make it easy for them to take the leap: either way, they are on their own. Many individuals find themselves on the edge of an abyss, trying to make a decision to act and are frightened to jump. When all is said and done, they are alone in either suffering the guilt of not acting or suffering the anxiety of acting:

The answer must therefore be: You're on your own – just jump! Either that or stay the same.

If company politics are to be confronted it must be every individual's, every manager's and every senior executive's project to accept personal responsibility for the moral challenge of confronting unacceptable behaviour. By making appropriate decisions they can create their own happiness, sense of achievement, satisfaction and personal development

Many people will say: 'OK you've convinced me so, How do I do it?'

How do I do it?

The answer is simple: keep taking the risks of crossing your Rubicon! That's all there is – JUMP! And then people say 'Yeah, but how do I do it?'! Personal change is never easy. When people ask for a simple answer to the problem of change, I am reminded of this lovely anecdote that was given to me by my friend and colleague, Peter Cockman:

Then Jesus took his disciples up the mountain and gathering them around him, he taught them, saying:

Blessed are the poor in spirit for theirs is the kingdom of heaven.
Blessed are the meek.
Blessed are they that mourn.
Blessed are the merciful.
Blessed are they that thirst for justice.
Blessed are you when you are persecuted.
Blessed are you when you suffer,
Be glad and rejoice for your reward is great in heaven.

Then Simon and Peter said, *Are we supposed to know this?*
And Andrew said, *Do we have to write this down?*
And James said, *Will we have a test on this?*
And Philip said, *Does this count?*
And Bartholomew said, *Do we have to hand this in?*
And John said, *The other disciples didn't have to learn this.*
And Matthew said, *Can I go to the toilet?*
And Judas said, *What does this have to do with real life?*

Then one of the Pharisees who was present asked to see Jesus' lesson plan and inquired of Jesus:

Where is your anticipatory set and your objectives in the cognitive domain?

And Jesus wept.

Many individuals come to a learning experience expecting to find something definite, something permanent, something unchanging upon which to depend. We look to the 'expert' to provide the solution, a system of thought or frame of reference. Their personal awareness of their own answers and of choosing have been numbed in school at a very early age:

> **'** As a rule, the individual . . . fails to see his own potentialities for decision. Instead he is constantly and anxiously looking around for external rules and regulations which can guide him in his perplexity . . . a good deal of the blame for this rests with education which promulgates the old generalisations and says nothing about the secrets of private experience.**'** *(Jung, 1961, p. 62)*

Indeed, when the individual tries to assert a personal view on anything he is made to feel he is somehow 'naughty' or uncouth. In the same way, attempts to change cultures have generally begun by specifying the dispositions that the leaders value and intend to reinforce through rewards and punishments, such as a 'customer-first' mentality, honest and open teamworking and interdepartmental cooperation. As Jung (1963), put it:

> **'** Every effort is made to teach idealistic beliefs or conduct which people know in their hearts they can never live up to, and such ideals are preached by officials who know that they themselves have never lived up to these high standards and never will. What is more, nobody ever questions the value of this kind of teaching.**'** *(p. 62)*

It's time it was questioned, since demonstrably it hasn't worked. Most continue to say one thing and do another. And when this has not worked everyone points the finger. So what is the alternative?

Existential education

Existentialism offers instead a reflection that life is just what it seems to be – a changing, ambiguous, ephemeral mixed bag. A whole new understanding of authority and 'truth' is needed, whereby the learner's feelings towards authority and 'truth' is as important as his cognitive understanding of it. Kopp (1972) sums it up:

> ❝ the Zaddick [Hassidic guru] instructs . . . by indirection, not by teaching, the pilgrims to be more like him, but to be more like themselves.❞ *(p. 11)*

For example, a workshop can be seen as a microcosm of the culture the organisation is trying to create, with the mutually agreed contract in Chapter 2 which includes such things as: 'Share in decision making,' 'Raise issues as and when they arise', and 'Say what you mean'. If it is *mutually* agreed that the group breaks for lunch at 1 o'clock and at 1.20 they are still talking, some individuals seek to blame the leader, some say nothing and some look in a disgruntled fashion at their watches. Conventionally, the leader might be defensive and either apologise or blame the others. Either way the conversation will be about time management and who was responsible for it.

The existential approach would be to refer back to the mutually agreed contract and raise awareness of such issues as:

(a) Saying one thing by agreeing to a contract and doing another by reneging on the decision (*shallow agreements and broken commitments*)

(b) The habitual response which is to blame the leader (*blame others*)

(c) The different styles of dealing with this dependency on the leader such as silence, non-verbal cues or blaming loudly (*counterdependency and dependency*)

(d) Relating these authority issues and their response when things don't go the way they expected to examples back in their everyday working practices (*seeing mistakes as terrible rather than as a learning experience*)

(e) Not taking personal responsibility for changing the culture by sticking to the new contract and acting accordingly, no matter how risky it is (*not raising issues as and when they arise*).

The role of the existential leader is to use the content issues as a background to discuss each individual's attitudes to personal responsibility, dependency, choice, authority, truth, decision and so on and how these affect the dynamics of the group be it the workshop, the team, the department or the organisation.

In the above case, once the lunch break 'mistake' became a group issue:

- Some remained focused on the task
- Some were blaming the leader
- Some silently avoided the risk of acting and opted out
- Some hoped someone else would save them
- Some belatedly took the risk of speaking out.

Each example of not sticking to an explicit contract illustrates how each group member is responsible for the escalatation of company politics into a culture of non-cooperation as a result of the habitual way he deals with his situation when things go wrong. In other words, as Kneller (1958) puts it:

> ‘subjects are only tools for the realisation of subjectivity.’ (*p. 63*)

Education must awaken existential awareness in each individual which manifests itself most clearly in the awareness of *choosing*. Individuals are faced throughout their lives with agonising decisions and moral choices, some large and highly significant, others smaller and less so, but individuals have to recognise that, irrespective of their apparent significance, they define themselves by the choices they have made: that in fact they are the *sum total of their choices*. This awareness of themselves as the creator of their values, attitudes, behaviours and situation is sometimes painful, sometimes exhilarating.

But why not simply give them the theory that would help them to develop themselves? Because what is to be learned is 'too elusively simple to be grasped without *struggle, surrender*, and *experiencing* of how it is' (Kopp, 1972, p. 4).

A favourite method of Zen guidance is the use of the Koan, a problem that is insoluble by conventional or intellectual means. The pilgrim must struggle until either he *gives up* in despair or *gives in* and is enlightened. A classic example is to concentrate on the 'sound of one hand clapping'. Such problems are offered in response to the demands of young monks for clarification, the very demands with which they confuse themselves:

> • Thus, when they ask "How can I ever get emancipated?" the Zen Master may answer: "Who has ever put you in bondage?" •
> *(Suzuki, 1960, p. 106)*

Our attempts to *catch hold of what we are seeking* may prevent us from discovering what is already there.

> Benoit (1959, p. 175) describes an image of the man who imagines himself to be a prisoner in a cell. He stands at one end of the small, dark empty room, on his toes, with his arms stretched upwards, hands grasping a small barred window for support, the room's only apparent source of light. If he holds on tight, straining towards the window, head turned just so, he can see a bit of bright sunlight between the very top bars. So committed is his effort not to lose sight of that glimmer of life-giving light that it never occurs to him to let go and explore the darkness of the rest of the cell. So it is that he never discovers that the door at the other end of the cell is open, he is, in fact, free. He has always been free to walk out into the brightness of day, if only he would let go:
>
> > • [In life], we are defeated not only by the narrowness of our perspective, and our fear of the darkness, but by our excuses as well . . . we make circumstances our prison and other people our jailers. • *(Kopp, 1972, p. 143)*

The point is that it's lonely, it's painful, it's tough, it's never ending and It's it! There isn't any more. The phrase 'life is a journey' has been well and truly reiterated lately but the *pain of travelling alone* has not.

And still people say: 'Yes, but how do I do it?'

> And still people say: 'Yes, but how do I do it?'! Even if I said: 'Come
> and see me on Thursday at 2.00 p.m. and we'll talk for an hour and
> discover your hidden blocks and surface them.'
>
> They'd say: 'Yes, but how do I do that?' So I'd say: 'Well, we need
> to get to understand your suppressed fears, wishes and wants, the
> buttons people push, how you defend yourself against the pain of
> looking foolish, the payoffs and downside of this behaviour,
> appreciate the anxiety associated with action', and they'd interrupt
> and say: 'Yes, but how do I do it?'

What they mean is: 'I don't want to work at it – I want you to give me an
instant solution, a pill, a panacea.' There are no solutions out there.
Nobody has the whole truth – not Newton, not Einstein and probably
not Chaos Theory. The way we view our world is more about the
Zeitgeist than anything about the truth.

Just as in IT, it's no good asking for a packaged solution. Each
individual has to build their own system, customised to their individual
needs. And that takes time and effort. Until they're prepared to solve
their own problems regarding their existence and how they live their life,
nothing will change.

There is no Given, no Guru, no Zaddick, no Buddha, no Authority, no
Manager, just YOU. This book has provided some of the tools for
change. Individuals can hold each other's hand in a kind of heroic
partnership to give each other confidence but *it's like bungy jumping*,
someone can show you how to secure yourself, tell you what to do, how it
will feel, the best technique to avoid damaging yourself and even hold
your hand before you go, but in the final analysis *you and you alone must
jump*. Its experiential – you have to go through the pain alone. No one
can *live your life* for you any more than anyone can *die for you*.

In sum

From stress management to presentation skills to culture change, from
developing entrepreneurs and intrapreneurs, to assertiveness training,
teambuilding and confronting company politics – all these behaviours are

influenced by our management of our ego and our existential anxieties and fears. By confronting them and understanding them we can choose to change them. This existential-humanistic approach will facilitate the development of long-term culture change, increased profitability and company effectiveness by addressing those issues that the humanistic approach alone just doesn't address.

Change programmes need to focus on awakening each individual to their personal responsibility both for *their own situation* at work and for their very *desire to run away from their responsibility for it.* For those who feel their life is somehow unfair, unjust or messed up by others it's good to remember that:

Life is not about getting what you want, it's about meeting the challenges on the way.

It's about crossing Rubicons, forever. . .

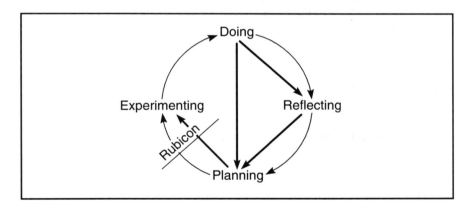

References

1 Is Company Politics Strangling Your Business, and You with It?

Wheelis, A., 'Will & Psychoanalysis', *Journal of Psychoanalytic Association*, 4 (1956).

2 Can Personal Responsibility be a 'Detachable Burden'?

Bierce, A., *The Devil's Dictionary* (Oxford Book of Quotations) (London: Penguin Books, 1976) Text No. 803.

Sartre, J.-P., *Existentialism*, (1947), cited in *International Thesaurus of Quotations* (London: Penguin Books, 1976) Text No. 315.

Rabbi Susya, cited in Friedman, M., *Introduction to Martin Buber: Between Man and Man* (New York: Macmillan, 1965).

3 Why Play Politics and Why Acquiesce?

Buber, M., *I and Thou* (New York: Charles Scribner, 1970).

4 Taking Action in a Hostile Environment

Coleman, J. C. and Hammen, C. L., *Contemporary Psychology and Effective Behaviour* (Glen View Illinois: Scott Foresman & Co., 1974).

Frankl, V. E., *Man's Search for Meaning* (Boston: Beacon Press, 1962).

Heidegger, M., *Being and Time* (New York: Harper & Row, 1962).

Kierkegaard, S., *Philosophical Fragments* (Princeton New Jersey: Princeton University Press, 1962).

Laing, R. D., *The Politics of Experience* and *The Bird of Paradise* (Harmondsworth, Middlesex: Penguin, 1967).

Maslow, A. H., *Motivation and Personality* (New York: Harper & Row, 1954).

Maslow, A. H., cited in 'Psychosources', *Psychology Resource Catalogue* (New York: Bantam, 1973).

May, R., *Love & Will* (New York: Basic Books, 1953).

Morris, V. C., *Existentialism in Education* (New York: Harper & Row, 1966).

Perls, F. S., *Gestalt Therapy Verbatim* (New York: Bantam Books, 1971).
Rogers, C. R., *On Becoming a Person* (Boston: Houghton Mifflin, 1970).
Sartre, J.-P., *No Exit and Three Other Plays* (New York: Vintage Books, 1955).
Sartre, J.-P., *Being and Nothingness*, trans. Hazel Barnes (New York: Philosophical Library, 1956).

5 Am I an Existentialist?

Kopp, S., *If you meet the Buddha on the road, kill him!* (London: Sheldon Press, 1972).
Fromm, E., *Escape from Freedom* (New York: Holt, Rinehart & Winston, 1941).
Kafka, F., *The Trial* (London: Minerva, 1992).
Morris, V. C., *Existentialism in Education* (New York: Harper & Row, 1966).
Perls, F. S., *Gestalt Therapy Verbatim* (New York: Bantam Books, 1971).
Pirsig, R. M., *Zen and the Art of Motor Cycle Maintenance* (London: Corgi Books, 1974).
Sartre, J.-P., *No Exit and Three Other Plays* (New York: Vintage Books, 1955).

6 If Freedom of Choice is Only 'an Illusion', Why Encourage Autonomy?

Freud, S., cited in R. May, *Love and Will* (New York: Basic Books, 1953).
May, R., *The Discovery of Being: Writings in Existential Psychology* (New York: Norton, 1959).
McGregor, D., *The Human Side of Enterprise* (New York: McGraw Hill, 1960).
Skinner, B. F., *Walden Two* (New York: Macmillan, 1948).
Skinner, B. F., *Science and Human Behaviour* (New York: Macmillan, 1953).
Skinner, B. F., *Beyond Freedom and Dignity* (New York: Alfred A. Knopf, 1971).
Rogers, C. R. and Skinner, B. F., 'Some Issues Concerning the Control of Human Behaviour: A Symposium', *Science*, 124 (1956), 1057–66.

7 Confronting the Cycle of Group Dynamics and Company Politics

Adair, J., *Effective Leadership* (London: Pan Books, 1983).
Blake, R. and Mouton, J., *Consultation*, 2nd edn (Reading, MA: Addison-Wesley, 1983).

8 How Does Company Politics Start?

Ellis, A., *Growth Through Reason* (Hollywood, CA: Wilshire Books, 1971).
Houston, G., *The Red Book of Groups* (London: The Rochester Foundation, 1984).

9 The Phenomenological Approach and Action

Bransford, J. D. and Johnson, M. K., 'Consideration of Some Problems of Comprehension', in W. G. Chase (ed.), *Visual Information Processing* (New York: Academic Press, 1973).
de Bono, E., *Textbook of Wisdom* (London: Viking, 1996).
Kant, I., *Critique of Pure Reason* (London: Everyman, 1993).

10 We Hypnotise Ourselves with Our Own Language

Ellis, A., *Growth Through Reason* (Hollywood, CA: Wilshire Books, 1971).
Rotter, J., 'Generalised Expectancies for Internal versus External Control of Reinforcement', *Psychological Monographs* 80 (1966).
Yalom, I. D., *Existential Psychotherapy* (New York: Basic Books, 1980).

11 Confronting Politics – The Stress of Inaction – The Anxiety of Action

Perls, F. S., *Gestalt Therapy Verbatim* (New York: Bantam Books, 1971).
Perls, F. S., Hefferline R. F. and Goodman, P., *Gestalt Therapy* (Harmondsworth: Penguin Books, 1951).

13 The Conflict is Within, not Without

Farber, L., *The Ways of the Will* (New York: Basic Books, 1966).
James, C., *The Silver Castle* (London: Random House, 1996).
Melden, A. L., *Free Action* (London: Routledge & Kegan Paul, 1961).
Perls, F. S., *Gestalt Therapy Verbatim* (New York: Bantam Books, 1971).
Perls, F. S., Hefferline R. F. and Goodman, P., *Gestalt Therapy* (Harmondsworth: Penguin Books, 1951).
Yalom, I. D., *Existential Psychotherapy* (New York: Basic Books, 1980).

14 So Your Indecision is Final?

Beckett, S., *Waiting for Godot* (London: Faber & Faber, 1956).
Camus, A., *The Stranger* (New York: Alfred A. Knopf, 1946).
Gardner, J., *Grendel* (London: Robin Clark, 1971).
Kafka, F., *Metamorphosis* (London: Mandarin, 1992).
Lodge, D., *Therapy* (Harmondsworth: Penguin Books, 1996).
Perls, F. S., Hefferline R. F. and Goodman, P., *Gestalt Therapy* (Harmondsworth: Penguin Books, 1951).

Sartre, J.-P., *Nausea* (Harmondsworth: Penguin Books, 1965).
Taubman, S., *Ending the Struggle against Yourself* (New York: Putnam's, 1994).
Wheelis, A., 'Will & Psychoanalysis', *Journal of Psychoanalytic Association*, 4 (1956).
Yalom, I. D., *Existential Psychotherapy* (New York: Basic Books, 1980).

15 How do I do it?

Benoit, H., *The Supreme Doctrine: Psychological Studies in Zen Thought* (New York: The Viking Press, 1959).
Jung, C. G., *Memories, Dreams, Reflections* (New York: Pantheon Books, 1963).
Kneller, G. F., *Existentialism and Education* (New York: Philosophical Library, 1958).
Kopp, S., *If you meet Buddha on the road, kill him!* (London: Sheldon Press, 1972).
Suzuki, D., *Manual of Zen Buddhism* (New York: Grove Press, 1960).